To Valentine Hodge,
Rich blessing on yours
Today and forever

Enjoying Jesus.
Paul Gruen

Religious Kings in the Sheepfold

Paul Grier

LC LONGWOOD COMMUNICATIONS

Unless otherwise noted, all scripture quotations are
from the King James Version of the Bible.

The king's names and definitions used in this book are
taken from Strong's Exhaustive Concordance of the
Bible.

Published by:
Longwood Communications
397 Kingslake Dr.
DeBary, FL 32713
(904) 774-1991

To contact the author please write:
Paul Grier
Drawer 490
Bertram, TX 78605

M any have contributed to this book in different ways. While I have not directly quoted from other writers and teachers, I have been influenced by many.

At this time, I can only thank God for the Spirit of Truth, which has spoken through these individuals, because I am unsure of who said what.

One in particular who helped me greatly in Hebrew types and shadows is my long time friend, Don Hurley of Houston, Texas.

Thanks to Dennis Lindsay, Patti Conn, and the Christ For The Nations editorial staff for your labour of love in putting the book in order, and to Quin Sherrer, who was kind to encourage and answer my many questions about christian book writing.

Dr. and Mrs. Marvin Overton III have been of great encouragement and have played a large part in getting the book into print.

My deepest thanks to all of you! May the Lord richly bless you.

Religious Kings in the Sheepfold

Paul Grier is the third-generation member of the Church of Christ. In 1971, when he and his wife, Velda, received the baptism of the Holy Spirit in the bedroom of their East Texas home, their lives were drastically changed. Soon Paul and Velda, along with their two teenaged sons, left behind the comfort of their home, church, family and a prosperous business to begin full-time ministry.

In 1975, after one year of training and two years on staff at a Dallas Bible school, the Griers began to pastor and teach in Texas churches.

The revelation contained in this book was expanded upon and enriched through their experiences. In 1980 the family moved to Africa, teaching in Bible schools and at conferences. Their ministry has since spread to several other nations. The Griers' home base is now the Ambassadors for Christ Church in Burnet County in the Texas hill country.

Table of Contents

Religious Kings in the Sheepfold

This book is for those who have entered into the Spirit filled walk, and encountered resistance from an invisible enemy. If you are fully convinced that there is an angelic realm, both good and evil, and have been seeking revelation on this matter, then this may be the book for you.

Most interested will be those who have had frustrating experiences in finding true and lasting peace and unity in their church, their family, their nation.

It is our hope to reveal a fresh dimension of spiritual warfare by drawing a parallel between Joshua chapter 10, in which five Amorite kings joined together to attack Gideon and Israel, and the principalities, powers, rulers of darkness and spiritual wickedness in high places as mentioned in Ephesians 6:12. It is both exciting and necessary for those living in this present hour to experience a new dawning of revelation concerning spiritual warfare.

The reality of religious spirits who transform themselves as angels of light will be bibically explored. The next important thing to determine is where to start, and how to totally eradicate these spirits.

Scriptural depth as well as the practical steps necessary to accomplish goals as members of the victorious, overcoming Church, are found in this study. It is our hope that the subtle schemes of the enemy will be exposed by the light of Jesus Christ through the anointing of the Holy Spirit.

Chapter One

NONRELIGIOUS CHRISTIANITY

T he rain began to fall through the huge limbs of the giant oak tree under which we had gathered. Guitars strummed and young voices were singing, "Come by here, Lord, come by here."

Rachel, a young college student, prayed, "Jesus, You know that it is really, really important for us to be able to continue this meeting. You know what I mean? Like, we have gone through a bunch of hassles to get certain people here, and it would be a real bummer if we get rained out. Amen."

Immediately the rain stopped, as if a faucet had been shut off somewhere in the heavens. After shouts of joy, the songs began again. A few minutes later our singing was again interrupted by rain.

This time it was Bubba who said, "Now I don't know who's causing this rain, but I'm telling you right now to buzz off!"

As the rain suddenly stopped again, every eye was fixed on Ray, who was kneeling in the middle with his hands lifted to heaven. "Okay, Lord, I've seen enough!" Laughter rang out among the students, and they began to clap and dance around in circles.

What we did not know was that Ray was the religious skeptic on campus. He considered it his life's calling to harass all young Christians who believed in the Holy Spirit and miracles. The girls had enticed him to come with the promise of being in on a different kind of wild party.

As Holy Spirit praise began to flow through him, we realized that there was an alarming difference between institutional religion and what was happening here.

Questions bombarded our minds. Would God actually hear the prayers of people dressed in shorts and halters? Could our holy God respond to such language as bummer and hassle? Would Satan actually flee when told to buzz off? Was a field surrounded by a wooden fence out in the middle of a cow pasture a proper place of worship?

All this was theologically disturbing to a third-generation Church of Christ man and his wife. However, it began to dawn on us that maybe, for the first time in thirty years, we had just experienced nonreligious, Spirit-led worship.

Please, Don't Help Us Recover

Three weeks earlier, my wife, Velda, and I had received the baptism of the Holy Spirit in the bedroom of our East Texas home. What began with waves and waves of laughter went on for several days.

Our two teenaged sons began to agree with some of the brethren of our local congregation that possibly we were sick and needed to seek professional help. Through groans of "belly laughter," Velda and I pleaded, "Please, please, we want to stay sick!"

Several weeks later as I opened our liquor cabinet,

I realized that for the first time there was not the slightest need for alcohol in my life. Velda and I laughed and worshipped as we flushed Jack Daniels, Bud and his friends down the toilet.

Holy Spirit intoxication happened regularly among the youth as we met in homes, in outside gatherings and in youth camps. But seldom did it occur in religious places such as church auditoriums where there seemed to be spirits of bondage that would not allow it to happen. As long as we experienced these "Holy Spirit high times," none of the young people had any problems with alcohol or drugs. Unfortunately, within a few months parents and church leaders had forced the young people back into a religious mold, and the same old problems began again.

God has created in every person a need for the intoxicating comfort that only the Holy Spirit can provide. If this thirst is not quenched with the flow of Living Water, the new wine of God, a person will try all kinds of unholy ways to satisfy this need—dead religion, alcohol, drugs, sexual perversion and worldly entertainment. Ephesians 5:18 says, **"Do not get drunk on wine, which leads to debauchery. Instead, be filled with the Spirit"** (NIV).

The "Gift of Suspicion"

The next enlightenment the Holy Spirit had in store for us was the reality of the demonic world. It seemed that almost everyone we came into contact with had been into some form of the occult. And although they had been baptized in the Holy Spirit, they were still experiencing weird manifestations.

In our great zeal and lack of wisdom, God protected us during some hair-raising experiences. In those days, instead of having the discerning of spirits,

13

the "gift of suspicion" flowed freely. On one occasion, as we were feverishly rebuking what we thought was a demon, I opened my eyes to see a black substance running from this young girl's eyes, making ugly streaks down her face. Jumping back, I gasped to the brother who was ministering with me, "What kind of spirit is this?" With a disgusted frown, he said, "Mascara."

After finishing Bible college in Dallas, I became a staff member at the school. For two more years, I assisted daily in helping students get free from many different kinds of unclean spirits.

Religious Wars

It was after we began to pastor that we saw the reality of religious spirits at work—even in the midst of Christians who had been born again, baptized in water and in the Holy Spirit. Brothers and sisters who loved one another would at times become violent over religious issues.

I walked into a religious war as I took my first pastorate. Thirty Church of Christ members and their preacher had received the baptism of the Holy Spirit at the same time. They started their own congregation, which grew rapidly. A religious argument arose, physical violence was threatened, and one group locked the other out of the building. The police were called to restore order. The pastor and half the congregation left; the other half remained and began to look for a pastor. I zealously responded to the call. This was the beginning of two frustrating years of dealing with religious spirits.

The next church we accepted was much like the first, but the members were of a Baptist background. After struggling for three years, we asked God to send us to Africa. We thought surely we would escape these spirits of religious bondage there.

In Africa, some leaders of a major denomination left the organization and started their own ministries. Feeling they should be allowed to keep the buildings they had built while with the organization, war broke out—with knives and clubs and the burning of homes. Several were put into prison, and the incident became a national religious scandal. May I quickly add that not all African Christians have a waring spirit and not all Church of Christ or Baptist people need deliverance, but I am only relating our particular experiences in religious wars.

It seemed I could no longer escape, so I stayed and began to teach in Bible schools and leadership conferences on the subject of the blood covenant. It was during this time that it began to dawn on me how religious spirits counterfeit Jesus Christ, the Living Word, in the midst of the Church. When these spirits are in control, people cannot discern the difference between the flow of adrenaline and the movement of the Holy Spirit. Nor can they distinguish head knowledge from truth. They are always looking for a religious cause to promote or fight for, and they picture themselves as martyrs when resistance comes.

Most of the time, revelation comes to me through Scripture first; experience comes later. The reverse happened in this case. I was forced to search and pray for revelation. In the next chapter I will begin to share with you some of these scriptural foundations.

Chapter Two

BINDING THE KINGS

The primary scriptural text examined in this text is the book of Joshua. Like the Old Testament kings and nations that fought against Israel, so are the spiritual enemies of God mentioned in Ephesians 6:12:

For we wrestle not against flesh and blood, but against principalities, against powers, against the rulers of the darkness of this world, against spiritual wickedness in high places.

The battles recorded in the Old Testament are examples of spiritual warfare. We can learn the strategies employed and use them to defeat the spiritual enemies of God.

Wherefore Adonizedec king of Jerusalem sent unto Hoham king of Hebron, and unto Piram king of Jarmuth, and unto Japhia king of Lachish, and unto Debir king of Eglon, saying, Come up unto me, and help me, that we may smite Gibeon: for it hath made peace with Joshua and with the children of Israel (Josh. 10:3–4).

In this scripture we see five Amorite kings, driven

by great fear, joining together and warring against Gibeon because that city had made peace with Israel (a type for the Church). Our spiritual enemies fear unity in the body of Christ more than anything else. They assign their strongest and most subtle ruler spirits to try to keep the Church in disunity.

The meaning of the roots of the five king's names or the places over which they ruled indicate that the Kings are types of religious ruler spirits. Their names are legalism, sectarianism, lawlessness, rationalism and ritualism. We will devote a chapter to each of these spirits to find out how to discern, bind, tread upon and nail these spirits to the cross.

And it was told Joshua, saying, The five kings are found in a cave at Makkedah. And Joshua said, Roll great stones upon the mouth of the cave, and set men by it for to keep them: and stay ye not, but pursue after your enemies, and smite the hindmost of them; suffer them not to enter into their cities: for the Lord your God hath delivered them into your hand (Josh. 10:17–19).

Angels of Light

And no marvel; for Satan himself is transformed into an angel of light. Therefore it is no great thing if his ministers also be transformed as the ministers of righteousness; whose end shall be according to their works (2 Cor. 11:14–15).

The five kings started the battle and then hid in the cave of Makkedah. The Hebrew word *Makkedah* means "sheepfold, the place where sheep are gathered for branding." Makkedah is a type for the Church.

Some spirits disguise themselves as ministers of light in the midst of saints. Like the "big boss" of a drug ring, when the heat is on they go into hiding.

17

Some of the lesser members of the gang may be arrested, but the strong man is never bound.

Sometimes in spiritual warfare we deal with surface problems but never discern and deal with the root problem. A weed cannot be killed by cutting off one leaf at a time. The root must be exposed and severed.

Or else how can one enter into a strong man's house, and spoil his goods, except he first bind the strong man? and then he will spoil his house (Matt. 12:29).

Binding with the Rock of Revelation

The five kings were discovered hiding in the cave. Joshua (which means Jesus) had great stones rolled over the mouth of the cave. Then he assigned soldiers to keep them there while the rest of the army was chased down and destroyed.

When Jesus spoke to Peter concerning binding and loosing, He was referring to revelation knowledge. Such revelation is more than earthly knowledge—it is a spiritual rock against which the gates of hell cannot prevail.

And Simon Peter answered and said, **Thou art the Christ, the Son of the living God. And Jesus answered and said unto him, Blessed art thou, Simon Bar-jona: for flesh and blood hath not revealed it unto thee, but my Father which is in heaven. And I say also unto thee, That thou art Peter, and upon this rock I will build my church; and the gates of hell shall not prevail against it. And I will give unto thee the keys of the kingdom of heaven: and whatsoever thou shalt bind on earth shall be bound in heaven: and whatsoever thou shalt loose on earth shall be loosed in heaven (Matt. 16:16–19).**

When the strongman, or ruler spirit, is bound, the lesser in rank flee because they have no command from their king. Satan's army is motivated by fear. Just as God is love, Satan is fear. He is out to split our ranks and break our communication with Jesus, our commander, the Living Word. Therefore, it should be our aim to bind the ruler spirits, which will cause all those under their command to flee in confusion.

David bound the strongman, Goliath, with one rock from his sling. Only then did the Israelite army rally and chase the enemy to the gates of Ekron. The meaning of the Hebrew word *Ekron* is "extermination and eradication."

Judah—which means "praise that is lifted high like an arrow which is shot or a rock that is thrown" led this army. Holy Spirit praise must always be an important part of warfare. Once the strongman is bound, those who praise have the privilege of joining the chase. The purpose of Jesus' coming to earth was to give the Church power to completely destroy the works of the devil. We must not stop short of that.

He that committeth sin is of the devil; for the devil sinneth from the beginning. For this purpose the Son of God was manifested, that he might destroy the works of the devil (1 Jn. 3:8).

One way the works of the devil are destroyed is through the rock of revelation knowledge. It comes by the anointing, a spiritual intoxication, which flows when there is preaching and worship on a higher level than human reasoning. This binds spiritual kings of religious darkness who try to break the flow of this new wine anointing.

Let the high praises of God be in their mouth, and a two-edged sword in their hand; to execute vengeance upon the heathen, and punishments upon the people; to bind their kings with chains,

and their nobles with fetters of iron (Ps. 149:6–8).

As the gasoline lanterns flickered in the dimly lit hall of a mission station in southern Africa, I could see many laughing faces with beautiful white teeth. Wave after wave of laughter swept through this place in which one hundred African leaders, ten European missionaries and one Texas Bible teacher (me) had gathered for a three-day seminar. Black and white men were energetically hugging one another. Then, as if our knees and ankles had turned to jelly, we fell to the floor, rolling and laughing, unable to stand for several minutes.

It was my fifth trip to Africa as a conference speaker. After beginning the ninth session on the subject of binding religious spirits, the spirit of laughter came. It moved on a few at first; then like the wind, it swept through the entire gathering. It was similar to the day of Pentecost recorded in the second chapter of Acts. People of different nations, race and language appeared to be drunk from new wine. I knew something wonderful was happening, and I was not to direct it in any way.

The next day I learned what had really happened. The African council members and the European missionaries, with glowing faces, said, "We have cut a blood covenant just like Jonathan and David did, and have sworn that the Lord will watch between us forever." They admitted that only two days earlier, a decision had been made in an official meeting. After eighteen years, they had concurred that it was no longer possible for Europeans and Africans to work together—too many religious and cultural differences existed. Muto, the spokesman, said, "It was while we were lying on the floor, rolling with laughter, that all our differences became so small; we've forgotten what they were."

We have experienced similar manifestations in Germany, Zimbabwe and the United States. A spirit of reconciliation comes, overpowering the sectarian spirits of race, legalistic doctrine, ritualistic and rational thinking, lawlessness, even bridging generation gaps. The Holy Spirit can correct problems in one hour that man has not been able to solve for generations. It's difficult for a trained leader to step aside; but we must learn to allow the Holy Spirit to move in the manner He desires.

During my early years of pastoring, when this kind of manifestation would begin, I would quickly quench the Spirit for fear of losing control of the situation . Currently, these outpourings are not happening every time we meet. There is no predictability with regard to those events. One thing is certain: when these "new wine" experiences occur, the church is purged of religious spirits.

There are always those who protest, but they have two choices: they must go with God's flow or be removed by Him. Leadership must be prepared for purging, knowing that it is necessary for lasting increase. It is easy for me to sympathize with feelings of fear, because initially I felt the same way. Then I remembered all the prayers made for deliverance from the bondage of dead religion. So I responded, "Lord, bring it on, even if it's not the way I had in mind."

Why do the nations rage and the peoples plot in vain? The kings of the earth take their stand and the rulers gather together against the Lord and against his Anointed One. "Let us break their chains," they say, "and throw off their fetters." The One enthroned in heaven laughs; the Lord scoffs at them (Ps. 2:1–4).

When we are in the Spirit and we see God laughing and rejoicing over the enemy, we join in by

21

faith and see things from His vantage point.

The Territory of the Conflict

God revealed to Daniel a battle in heavenly places. It was a battle between the angels of God and the prince of Persia. This territory as we know it today is an arena for many wars. These wars are kingdom-against-kingdom conflicts inspired by religious spirits. Satan assigns each spirit a principality or kingdom to dominate. Lower-ranking spirits are assigned to possess individual bodies, but ruler spirits are assigned to dominate nations, cities, counties, church congregations or families. Or they may be assigned to the domains of finance, industry, science, politics, race, education, military, a list too long to mention each one.

Then said he unto me, Fear not, Daniel: for from the first day that thou didst set thine heart to understand, and to chasten thyself before thy God, thy words were heard, and I am come for thy words. But the prince of the kingdom of Persia withstood me one and twenty days: but, lo, Michael, one of the chief princes, came to help me; and I remained there with the kings of Persia. Now I am come to make thee understand what shall befall thy people in the latter days: for yet the vision is for many days (Dan. 10:12–14).

Deliverance for the Whole Territory

Individuals need to be set free, but whole congregations, nations, cities and families also need deliverance. It is my observation as a pastor that problems such as divorce, sickness, accidents, waves of depression, and others, often come in bunches–like bananas. If one person in a group is delivered, the spirit moves over to someone else in the same group. This was a great mystery to me until I understood the nature of ruler spirits.

A united congregation needs to first *discern* the ruler spirits—not reason with the natural mind—to get a solid rock word of revelation. Then, the assembly must bind the ruler spirits by speaking revelation under the anointing of the Holy Spirit. The ruler spirits not easily discerned are legalism, sectarianism, lawlessness, rationalism and ritualism. When these spirits are bound, it is easier to deal with those of lesser rank—divorce, sickness or rejection. Pride and fear are spirits of higher rank than religious spirits.

Band-Aid or Cure

In one of our congregations, there was a man who was a drunkard. His wife and children were very faithful. Many believers had prayed against the spirit of drunkenness and addiction but with no lasting results. He would drink for days in succession, and when he decided to stop, he would call me or come by my house. We would pray, and God would consistently sober him.

One night when he came over, he was incoherent. As he started to talk about his drinking problem, I heard myself saying something I had not considered before. "You don't have a drinking problem; you have a fear problem."

This man was one of the biggest and strongest men I had ever known. In the natural it seemed he was not afraid of anything. With a red face, he jumped to his feet, doubled up his fist and through clenched teeth screamed with a voice not his own, "Don't you ever tell anybody that!"

His wife was advised not to mention drunkenness

again but instead feed him scriptures on overcoming fear. I have since found this to be the case with most alcoholics and addicts. Spiritual warfare usually cannot be based on our natural senses.

Stay for Breakthrough

During corporate prayer or praise, sometimes there is a struggle at first. But it is important to stay with it until a breakthrough comes. When the enemy begins to flee, the entire congregation can feel it. There are shouts of victory and tears of joy. Singing in the spirit flows effortlessly, like waves of the ocean. Time becomes insignificant. A holy silence may follow that no one dares disturb. This is a time to listen with spiritual ears—anticipate the rest that comes after the release. Sometimes we quit too soon—just after the emotional high. When the enemy is on the run, it is essential to keep up the chase.

Moses stayed for six days in the midst of God's mighty demonstration of power before he ever heard one word of the Ten Commandments. It was not in the thunder and lightning or rock-splitting wind that Elijah heard God but in a still, small voice. Clocks and calendars are enemies to be conquered in this type of warfare.

There is a league in Satan's army united by fear. One ruler of darkness does not attempt anything alone; he enlists others to help, as in the case of the five kings in Joshua 10. That is the reason it is absolutely necessary for there to be true unified action in the Church.

The pressures of life drive us to pray in tongues—in a language beyond our understanding. Praying and singing in tongues with others has become a necessity for me. It is in that atmosphere that prophetic utterances come to confirm the written Word, solutions to unsolvable problems become clear, and we are lifted into a higher place in the Spirit.

I am assuming you have experienced these things. If not, please stop right now and ask Jesus to baptize you in the Holy Spirit. Open your mouth and allow the Spirit to speak in a language unknown to your natural mind.

Chapter Three

SPIRIT OF LEGALISM
(ADONIZEDEC, KING OF JERUSALEM)

THe five kings of the Amorites, the king of Jerusalem, the king of Hebron, the king of Jarmuth, the king of Lachish, the king of Eglon, gathered themselves together, and went up, they and all their hosts, and encamped before Gibeon, and made war against it (Josh. 10:3–5).

In King Adonizedek we see the spirit of legalism that operates in many institutions today. It surfaces in every generation wearing different clothing. The meaning of *Adonizedek* is "lord of justice, ruler and sovereign controller."

This spirit seeks to use the letter of the law to bind the Church in the name of justice. It disregards grace, mercy and liberty, which were purchased by the blood of Jesus.

The Sport of Legalistic Debate

In the church I belonged to for the first twenty years of my life, legalistic debating was a lifestyle. Somehow our thinking had become perverted; in our minds, witnessing was enticing someone to argue over a scripture and then "nailing him." Looking back, I realize it was a kind of sport with a reward—bragging rites. We never listened to others because we were too busy thinking of a comeback.

Sometimes folks become intoxicated on their own adrenaline (as previously mentioned) and think it is the Holy Spirit. This opens the door to a legalistic demon of debate. Those who think this spirit can be overcome through natural knowledge or who mouth religious cliches do not understand what they are up against. To have authority over devils we must use spiritual weapons. Religious debate is useless.

When I led my first Wednesday night discussion class, everyone present knew the Bible better than I. This class had gone through a series of leaders over many years and were now desirous of "fresh meat" and I don't mean the meat of the Word.

In self-defense, I began to earnestly study the Bible for the first time. In desperation, I asked God to show me truth. The favorite saying in this church was, "We have the truth." As I studied, I was shocked to see the differences between what I had been taught and what I was seeing in the Word, especially about the Holy Spirit.

I was teaching out of the Book of Acts and the Holy Spirit would come over me as I taught. Some of the things I said would leave the members of the class speechless. I didn't understand why, but I knew I liked it. I lasted two years; then I was replaced. I felt blessed that I had not been stoned like Stephen. (Several did run out of the building with hands over their ears, literally gnashing their teeth.)

During heated debates over scriptural issues, anger can take root in those expressing extreme views. Sometimes the ruler spirit of legalism opens the door to a spirit of murder. This applies both naturally and spiritually.

The Letter Kills

When we speak of law or legalism, people immediately think of the Old Testament law of Moses. But New Testament "letter of the law" Scripture can also be used to prove a point.

Who also hath made us able ministers of the new testament; not of the letter, but of the spirit: for the letter killeth, but the spirit giveth life (2 Cor. 3:6).

Churches in our denomination have split over communion cups—whether to take communion wine from many different cups or from one, since Jesus took THE cup at the Last Supper (see Matt. 26:27). Another issue that has caused division is instrumental music in worship. The controversy was over Ephesians 5:19: "Sing and make music in your heart to the Lord" (NIV). The legalism of others may seem funny, But wait until the Holy Spirit points out yours; it's not such a laughing matter then.

A Bewitching Spirit

Legalism is a spiritual problem, not a rational one. Overcoming legalism requires spiritual weapons; reasoning is futile.

O foolish Galatians, who hath bewitched you, that ye should not obey the truth, before whose eyes Jesus Christ hath been evidently set forth, crucified among you? This only would I learn of you, Received ye the Spirit by the works of the law, or by the hearing of faith? (Gal. 3:1–2).

The word *bewitched* means "under a demonic

28

spell." The early Church was not only troubled by wrong thinking but by a religious devil called *law*. This spirit still seeks to control the minds of Christians so they cannot discern truth. The law of justice replaces mercy and becomes the lord or ruling spirit in a congregation. An attorney who searches for the point of law that proves his case is not necessarily interested in the truth. A church dominated by a spirit of legalism is the same.

A spirit of legalism inhabits an institutional framework rather than an individual. It moves from member to member, seeking to establish unity around legalities rather than truth. Pride surfaces as members flaunt their knowledge of the Bible. Every Christian is faced with the same choice Adam and Eve were in the Garden: the tree of life or the tree of the knowledge of good and evil.

Remember, Satan can quote scripture for his purposes. He used Psalm 91:11–12 while tempting Jesus:

And he brought him to Jerusalem, and set him on a pinnacle of the temple, and said unto him, If thou be the Son of God, cast thyself down from hence: for it is written, He shall give his angels charge over thee, to keep thee: and in their hands they shall bear thee up, lest at any time thou dash thy foot against a stone (Luke 4:9–11).

Devils believe the Scriptures but refuse to act upon their knowledge. This is dead or religious faith and is a doctrine of devils.

Thou believest that there is one God; thou doest well: the devils also believe, and tremble. But wilt thou know, O vain man, that faith without works is dead? (James 2:19–20).

Since a spirit of legalism impersonates the Spirit of Truth, it cannot be easily discerned. A seducing spirit inserts just enough scriptural fact to deceive Christians who have a little knowledge of the Bible.

Now the Spirit speaketh expressly, that in the latter times some shall depart from the faith, giving heed to seducing spirits, and doctrines of devils (1 Tim. 4:1).

The Jerusalem Board Meeting

During the ministry of Paul and Barnabas recorded in Acts 15, some Christian Jews taught that unless a gentile was circumcised, he could not be saved. This caused a great deal of dissension and dispute. It was decided that Paul, Barnabas and others should go to Jerusalem to confer with the apostles and elders about the question. In Jerusalem there was more debating and contending. When the spirit of legalism is operating, the object is not to find the truth. The object is to win the battle so that one's personal pride can remain intact.

People Must Have Their Say

Usually, people want to have their say before they will listen to the Holy Spirit. At one time I owned a television service company. Almost every day I had to listen to complaints. In my earlier days, I often became defensive and told the customer he was wrong. As I became more experienced, I realized that the customer just wanted to have his say. After listening I would ask, "What can we do to correct this matter for you?" Without fail, they would reply, "Nothing, really. I just wanted you to know how I felt about it."

Letting others have their say is difficult and requires supernatural self-control. The only way the dispute in Acts 15 was settled was by waiting upon the Spirit and allowing Him to speak.

Then pleased it the apostles and elders, with the whole church, to send chosen men of their own company to Antioch with Paul and Barnabas; namely, Judas surnamed Barsabas, and Silas, chief men among the brethren. . . . For it seemed good to the Holy Ghost, and to us, to lay upon you no greater burden than these necessary things; that ye abstain from meats offered to idols, and from blood, and from things strangled, and from fornication: from which if ye keep yourselves, ye shall do well. Fare ye well (Acts 15:22, 28–29).

The Law of Liberty

Notice the liberty this decision brought. The Jewish Christians were free to practice circumcision and be blessed. The gentiles were free not to circumcise. Yet at the same time there were absolutes that applied to both. Only the Spirit of God could come up with such an all-inclusive plan.

Who art thou that judgest another man's servant? to his own master he standeth or falleth. Yea, he shall be holden up: for God is able to make him stand. One man esteemeth one day above another: another esteemeth every day alike. Let every man be fully persuaded in his own mind (Rom. 14:4–5).

For with what judgment ye judge, ye shall be judged: and with what measure ye mete, it shall be measured to you again (Matt. 7:2).

Now the Lord is that Spirit: and where the Spirit of the Lord is, there is liberty (2 Cor. 3:17).

When Velda and I first received the baptism of the Holy Spirit after thirty years of religious bondage, we were like birds released from a cage. We were so free! Some say their initial evidence of the Holy Spirit was tongues, but ours was not having to suffer through Sunday night services. We just drove around and laughed and laughed with no condemnation. (Later God dealt with us about lawlessness, which is covered in another chapter.)

Jesus—Our Example

Jesus gave us the perfect example of how to use spiritual warfare in the way that He dealt with the scribes, lawyers, Pharisees and Sadducees. He never debated; He responded with a spiritual rock, binding their religious arguments. The only reason for their words was to find something to use against Him.

Ye blind guides, which strain at a gnat, and swallow a camel (Matt. 23:24).

Woe unto you, lawyers! for ye have taken away the key of knowledge: ye entered not in yourselves, and them that were entering in ye hindered. And as he said these things unto them, the scribes and the Pharisees began to urge him vehemently, and to provoke him to speak of many things: laying wait for him, and seeking to catch something out of his mouth, that they might accuse him (Luke 11:52–54).

As we mature, our words should become fewer and the manifestation of power increase. Someone said, "A person with an experience is never at the mercy of one who only has an argument." Jesus backed up what He said with powerful signs. Should it be any different today?

And when he was departed thence, he went into their synagogue: and, behold, there was a man which had his hand withered. And they asked him, saying, Is it lawful to heal on the sabbath days? that they might accuse him. And he said unto them,

What man shall there be among you, that shall have one sheep, and if it fall into a pit on the sabbath day, will he not lay hold on it, and lift it out? How much then is a man better than a sheep? Wherefore it is lawful to do well on the sabbath days. Then saith he to the man, Stretch forth thine hand. And he stretched it forth; and it was restored whole, like as the other. Then the Pharisees went out, and held a council against him, how they might destroy him. But when Jesus knew it, he withdrew himself from thence: and great multitudes followed him, and he healed them all (Matt. 12:9–15).

Deliverance from Satan Worship

At one of the Bible colleges where I worked, a Satan worshipper was brought for deliverance. She said she wanted to be set free and become a Christian. A young student was the only one available to assist me in ministering to her. (Remember, Satanism is a religion ruled by religious spirits.)

As we began to claim the authority of the blood of Jesus and speak the Word, she became violent. In a voice that was not her own, she began cursing and threatening, "Oh, I would like to kill you!" Snatching my Bible, she threw it against the wall, screaming, "I hate that book." This continued for about one hour as we declared the power of the blood and commanded the spirit to go in the name of Jesus.

Knowing that it should not take this long to obtain results, I asked the woman why she was not willing to be delivered. She replied that she had power to work miracles in the name of Satan. I heard myself saying, "The power in me is greater than the power of Satan."

I immediately began thinking I should not have said that, because I felt very powerless at that moment. But the

33

Spirit had spoken the truth through my lips, so without feeling power, I put my hands on her head. She jerked away and screamed, "What is wrong with your hands?"

Feeling very intimated, I looked at my hands to see if I had forgotten to wash them.

Again, I heard myself say, "This is the power I told you about." I put my hands back on her head. She fell over as if she were dead and lay there for about five minutes. Then, with a glorious glow about her, she rose to her feet and in a normal voice declared, "Jesus Christ is the Son of God." We left that place knowing it was not our words that set her free, but the rock of revelation spoken through weak and trembling lips.

The promise has been given that signs will follow those who believe and speak the words given by the Holy Spirit. Words alone do not bind ruler spirits of darkness. There must be a demonstration of power under the direction of God.

But if I with the finger of God cast out devils, no doubt the kingdom of God is come upon you (Luke 11:20).

If we are to be effective in spiritual warfare, we must learn to only say what the Spirit says. This is the two-edged sword—the rock that binds. It is not flesh and blood against the devil; it is kingdom against kingdom.

Jesus Uncovered Religious Spirits

It seems Jesus purposely did things in nonreligious ways to cause religious spirits to surface. One case in particular was the healing of the blind man's eyes.

And it was the sabbath day when Jesus made the clay, and opened his eyes. Then again the Pharisees also asked him how he had received his sight. He said unto them, He put clay upon mine

eyes, and I washed, and do see. Therefore said some of the Pharisees, This man is not of God, because he keepeth not the sabbath day. Others said, How can a man that is a sinner do such miracles? And there was a division among them (John 9:14–16).

Take note how this divided the spirits of religious bondage. "Any kingdom divided against itself shall not stand" (Matt. 12:25).

Jesus Spit In The Face of the Spirit of Blindness

And he took the blind man by the hand, and led him out of the town; and when he had spit on his eyes, and put his hands upon him, he asked him if he saw ought (Mark 8:23).

When Jesus spit on the blind man's eyes, I believe he was dealing with a spirit of blindness. The strongest rebuke to devils is to have the Word of God spit in their face under the anointing of the Holy Spirit. Today Jesus is not here in the flesh, but the Spirit-breathed Word can be used to rebuke every kind of devil.

Religious Spirits Hinder Healing

Often Christians who cannot receive healing are bound by a legalistic spirit. They think there is only one way healing can be administered, as did Naaman, the leper.

But Naaman was wroth, and went away, and said, Behold, I thought, He will surely come out to me, and stand, and call on the name of the Lord his God, and strike his hand over the place, and recover the leper (2 Kings 5:11).

His servants bound that legalistic spirit with an anointed word of exhortation which broke down Naaman's argument and led to his obedience.

And his servants came near, and spake unto him, and said, My father, if the prophet had bid thee do some great thing, wouldest thou not have done it? how much rather then, when he saith to thee, Wash, and be clean? (2 Kings 5:13).

When praying for the sick, the Holy Spirit has often prompted me to bind the religious spirits before rebuking the spirit of sickness. Only recently have I obeyed this because of my lack of understanding of these ruler spirits. As I have obeyed, the results have improved. People often get indignant when a religious spirit is mentioned. This is a good indication that the discernment was correct. It also points out the need for training on this type of spiritual warfare.

Holy Spirit Baptism is not the Automatic Cure-all

Upon entering Pentecostal, full gospel and independent charismatic circles, we were shocked to find the same legalistic spirits working—only over different issues.

Everyone is entitled to his or her own convictions on these matters. But it becomes sin when we bind them on others or break fellowship over them. Multitudes of Christians want the flow of the sweet Holy Spirit, not just another kind of legalism dressed in different clothing.

May we earnestly repent before Almighty God for being a stumbling block to the body of Christ. Let's place the rock of revelation knowledge upon the door of the Church. Renounce the spirit of legalism and go free in Jesus' name. Amen! Now, enter into the higher law of the spirit of the life of Christ Jesus.

For the law of the Spirit of life in Christ Jesus hath made me free from the law of sin and death (Rom. 8:2).

Chapter Four

SECTARIAN SPIRIT
(HOHAM, KING OF HEBRON)

Hebron, which was ruled by king Hoham, symbolizes the ruler spirit of sectarianism. Those under the influence of this spirit are convinced that their group is right and everyone else is wrong. The meaning of *Hebron* is "spell, enchantment, charmer; to fascinate; seat of association, a society; be compact, couple together, join self and league together."

Spirit of Bondage vs. Christ, the Mediator

The basis of sectarianism is demonic power. The foundation of the true Church is the blood covenant of Jesus Christ. We cannot link ourselves to the Church in the same way we join a club. It is possible to go through the motions of confession, baptism, catechism and other ordinances without being born again. But to the true Church, only the Lord adds members. We are saved by grace through faith and not by our works.

"And the Lord added to the church daily such as should be saved" (Acts 2:47).

37

The greatest miracle of all is to have our hearts knit together with Almighty Father God and the Body of Christ. This miracle will not happen by simply meeting qualifications laid out by an institution. Sectarian spirits are often the glue holding denominations, congregations, races, families, nations and fraternities together. But true unity comes only from God. Understanding Christ's role as mediator is crucial in determining the difference between the true spiritual body and a sect.

For there is one God, and one mediator between God and men, the man Christ Jesus (1 Tim. 2:5).

There can only be one binding power in the Church—Jesus Christ.

But now hath he obtained a more excellent ministry, by how much also he is the mediator of a better covenant, which was established upon better promises (Heb. 8:6). And for this cause he is the mediator of the new testament, that by means of death, for the redemption of the transgressions that were under the first testament, they which are called might receive the promise of eternal inheritance (Heb. 9:15).

Covenant with Abram

After God made His covenant with Abram, he refused Sodom's riches. Then God promised to be Abram's source of every supply. Abram believed the promise and was counted righteous. **And he believed in the Lord and he counted it to him for righteousness (Gen. 15:6).**

Later Abram wanted assurance that he would truly inherit the promise. And he said, **Lord God, whereby shall I know that I shall inherit it? (Gen. 15:8).** It was then that the mediator came into the picture. After

Abram had split the sacrificial animals down the middle (a type for Jesus' death), he fell into a deep sleep. At this time he saw Jesus as the mediator passing between blood-covered flesh in the form of a burning lamp and a smoking furnace.

And it came to pass, that, when the sun went down, and it was dark, behold a smoking furnace, and a burning lamp passed between those pieces (Gen. 15:17).

This vision represented the church, the glorious body of Christ: flesh covered by blood, with the Holy Spirit represented by light and the refining fire in the midst.

Your father Abraham rejoiced to see my day; and he saw it, and was glad (John 8:56).

In the Hebrew custom, two parties participated in a covenant equally. But Abram saw Jesus walking through death on behalf of him and his spiritual descendants. (We will go into more detail in a later chapter.)

Again I say unto you, That if two of you shall agree on earth as touching any thing that they shall ask, it shall be done for them of my Father which is in heaven. For where two or three are gathered together in my name, there am I in the midst of them (Matt. 18:19–20).

The Greek word *sunago* means "gathered together," as in verse 20. It means "to lead or drive together; collect or convene; union." To be in agreement with another does not necessarily mean the parties involved all have a democratic vote. In God's kingdom it means to be under the authority of the Father, Son and Holy Spirit, fully righteous—inwardly and outwardly—through the blood, the light and the fire.

39

Spirit of Unity—a Free Gift

Unity in the body is a gift of the Holy Spirit that man cannot fabricate. This gift is freely given, yet we are commanded to maintain unity through loving forbearance.

With all lowliness and meekness, with longsuffering, forbearing one another in love; endeavoring to keep the unity of the Spirit in the bond of peace (Eph. 4:2–3).

The church's unity was purchased for us on the cross when Christ allowed His bones to be dislocated by His own body weight. **I am poured out like water, and all my bones are out of joint; my heart is like wax; it is melted in the midst of my bowels (Ps. 22:14).**

Sects are formed around many different beliefs. But our confession is that Christ is in the midst of us. We do not need the bondage of man-made walls to hold us together.

Church creeds, constitutions and bylaws often dictate right and wrong rather than a daily yielding to the Holy Spirit. They are used as a party platform in a political context. This can give entrance to a sectarian spirit. The boundaries of spiritual fellowship cannot be set by anything man writes on paper. In churches where we have the oversight, we have constitutions and bylaws for the sake of state and federal government regulations, but it is made very clear that these do not spiritually govern the body.

The Greek definition for *sect* is "a party of disunion." If there is a spirit of union, it stands to reason that there is also a demon spirit of *dis*union that can only be bound with spiritual weapons.

Sectarian Spirit

Sectarian Indignation

Christians in bondage to a sectarian spirit become very indignant at healing and deliverance services. Even if they believe in healing and deliverance, unless it is performed in the name of their denomination or in accordance with their doctrinal statement, they scoff at it.

There came also a multitude out of the cities round about unto Jerusalem, bringing sick folks, and them which were vexed with unclean spirits: and they were healed every one. Then the high priest rose up, and all they that were with him, (which is the sect of the Sadducees) and were filled with indignation (Acts 5:16–17).

It's comforting to know that although John and the apostles were sometimes swayed by this spirit, Jesus still patiently loved and corrected them.

And John answered and said, Master, we saw one casting out devils in thy name; and we forbad him, because he followeth not with us. And Jesus said unto him, Forbid him not: for he that is not against us is for us. And it came to pass, when the time was come that he should be received up, he stedfastly set his face to go to Jerusalem, and sent messengers before his face: and they went, and entered into a village of the Samaritans, to make ready for him. And they did not receive him, because his face was as though he would go to Jerusalem. And when his disciples James and John saw this, they said, Lord, wilt thou that we command fire to come down from heaven, and consume them, even as Elias did? But he turned, and rebuked them, and said, Ye know not what manner of spirit ye are of (Luke 9:49–55).

Even today, Jesus will not let us call down fire nor condemn those who are doing the work of God apart from our group.

41

Man's Desire to Control

Like the apostles, we do not always recognize what spirit is in control. Sectarian spirits always want to "box in" the flow of the Holy Spirit. They are possessive and want to use the flow for selfish purposes.

A classic example of this is seen in the struggles between the herdsmen of King Abimelech and those of Isaac as recorded in Genesis 26. Because Isaac believed the covenant promise of God, he was greatly blessed. The Philistines envied him and stopped up the wells that his father, Abraham, had dug. Because of Isaac's success, the king considered him a threat to his kingdom and drove him away. Do you see the parallel with sectarian religion?

As Isaac's servants dug the wells again, they found "springing" or living water—a type for the flow of the Holy Spirit.

In the last day, that great day of the feast, Jesus stood and cried, saying, If any man thirst, let him come unto me, and drink. He that believeth on me, as the scripture hath said, out of his belly shall flow rivers of living water. (But this spake he of the Spirit, which they believe on him should receive: for the Holy Ghost was not yet given: because that Jesus was not yet glorified. (John 7:37–39).

Wells of Contention

And Isaac's servants digged in the valley, and found there a well of springing water. And the herdmen of Gerar did strive with Isaac's herdmen, saying, The water is ours: and he called the name of the well Esek; because they strove with him. And they digged another well, and strove for that also: and he called the name of it Sitnah (Gen. 26:19–21).

The Hebrew definition for *Esek* is "contention," and *Sitnah* means "hatred." The herdsmen of Gerar wanted to possess the flow in a sectarian way. There was plenty for everyone to share; yet they wanted to box, package and control it. This same spirit works undetected to drive well-meaning men who love God to grasp control with tightly clenched fists rather than opening their hands to all.

Heal the sick, cleanse the lepers, raise the dead, cast out devils: freely ye have received, freely give (Matt. 10:8).

It is my belief that the very people who have diligently prayed for the move of the Holy Spirit that is crossing all denominational boundaries today may also reject it when it does not happen exclusively within their framework and they will miss a great blessing.

The first manifestation of the sectarian spirit is contention. The second is hatred. We can try to cast them out of the individuals involved, but they seem to spring up in another place. It is an endless cycle until we discern the strongman ruler spirit and bind him with the Spirit-quickened Word of the blood covenant.

And he removed from thence, and digged another well; and for that they strove not: and he called the name of it Rehoboth; and he said, For now the Lord hath made room for us, and we shall be fruitful in the land (Gen. 26:22).

The name of this well is Rehoboth, which means "room." I liken this to those who grow tired of contention over the flow of the Spirit and choose to give themselves room. They become involved in independent fellowships or house meetings held at some time other than Sunday morning. However, this does not completely solve the problem. The Holy Spirit gives us the steps to take to ease the pressure. God blesses peacemakers by increasing the blessings for all to see (Matt.5:9).

Then Abimelech went to him from Gerar, and Ahuzzath one of his friends, and Phichol the chief captain of his army. And Isaac said unto them, Wherefore come ye to me, seeing ye hate me, and have sent me away from you? And they said, We saw certainly that the Lord was with thee: and we said, Let there be now an oath betwixt us, even betwixt us and thee, and let us make a covenant with thee; that thou wilt do us no hurt, as we have not touched thee, and as we have done unto thee nothing but good, and have sent thee away in peace; thou art now the blessed of the Lord. And he made them a feast, and they did eat and drink. And they rose up betimes in the morning, and sware one to another: and Isaac sent them away, and they departed from him in peace. And it came to pass the same day, that Isaac's servants came, and told him concerning the well which they had digged, and said unto him, We have found water. And he called it Shebah: therefore the name of the city is Beersheba unto this day (Gen. 26:26-33).

After seeing the ongoing covenant blessings of Isaac, the king and his captains asked him to enter into a blood covenant reconciliation with them. To wit, that God was in Christ, reconciling the world unto himself, not imputing their trespasses unto them; and hath committed unto us the word of reconciliation (II Cor.5:19).

Then said Jesus to them again, Peace be unto you: as my Father hath sent me, even so send I you. And when he had said this, he breathed on them, and saith unto them, Receive ye the Holy Ghost: whose soever sins yet remit, they are remitted unto them; and whose soever sins ye retain, they are retained (Jn. 20:21-23).

We are sent as ambassadors of peace in the same way the Father sent Jesus. We have been given power to speak words of forgiveness and to breathe forth the Holy Spirit in Jesus' name. It must be understood that "in His name" means we walk under His authority, not in our own self-will.

Isaac did not ask Abimelech to speak in tongues, go through Charismatic cathechism, nor sign a pledge card; they based their fellowship strictly on the blood covenant. The word "covenent" in Hebrew is beriyth which means to cut; a compact, league or confederacy made by passing between pieces of flesh. Although their covenant-making is not spelled out in detail, I believe they did what God commanded Abram to do in Genesis 15. Death through the shedding of blood must be the basis of any covenant for it to be a genuine binding contract.

This is why even the first covenant was not put into effect without blood. In fact, the law requires that nearly everything be cleansed with blood, and without the shedding of blood there is no forgiveness (see Heb. 9:18,22 NIV).

For the life of the flesh is in the blood: and I have given it to you upon the altar to make an atonement for your souls: for it is the blood that maketh an atonement for the soul (Lev. 17:11).

In the bread and wine in Genesis 26:30-31 we see a type of the Lord's Supper. Afterward, the partakers swore to one another, which is a type of our new and better covenant as recorded in Hebrews 6.

For when God made promise to Abraham, Because he could swear by no greater, he sware by himself, saying, Surely blessing I will bless thee, and multiplying I will multiply thee. And so, after he had patiently endured, he obtained the promise. For men verily swear by the greater: and an oath for confirmation is to them an end of all strife. Wherein God, willing more abundantly to shew

unto the heirs of promise the immutability of His counsel, confirmed it by an oath (Heb. 6 :13-17).

The promise of God is that if we, by faith, will accept Jesus as the mediator of the covenant, it will end all strife.

Notice that after cutting the covenant, the parties went their separate ways. Covenant relationship does not mean we need to be under the same roof, nor even in the same denomination or religious organization. Due to diversity of callings and gifts, people can covenant together even though they are in different churches or ministries.

One of my dearest brothers in the Lord was a leader in one of the churches we pastored. While we were trying to work together, we "fought like cats and dogs." Now that there are two hundred miles between us, we get along wonderfully. We visit each other about once a year and love the arrangement which God has worked out for us.

The last well was named Shebah, which means "the well of the oath." The flow of the fruit and gifts of the Spirit keep the body of Christ alive. This is a type of the life which flows through the blood.

Consider the spirit of antichrist. Anti means "something against or substitutionary" while the word Christ means "the anointing." Together they mean a spirit which is substitutionary to the flow of the Holy Spirit. Sectarian bondage is such a spirit.

Little children, it is the last time: and as ye have heard that antichrist shall come, even now are there many antichrists; whereby we know that it is the last time (1 Jn. 2:18).

But the anointing which ye have received of him abideth in you, and ye need not that any man teach you: but as the same anointing teacheth you of all things, and is truth, and is no lie, and even as it hath taught you, ye shall abide in him (I Jn. 2:27).

We are joined (covenanted) together through the flow which comes from Christ, the head, and flows through every joint.

But speaking the truth in love, may grow up into him in all things, which is the head, even Christ: from whom the whole body fitly joined together and compacted by that which every joint supplieth, according to the effectual working in the measure of every part, maketh increase of the body unto the edifying of itself in love (Eph. 4:15, 16).

Peter Overcomes A Sectarian Spirit

In Acts 10, Peter—who was a Jew—was sent by God to take the message of Christ to the gentiles, whom he considered unclean. Three times God commanded Peter not to count anything unclean which he had cleansed. Finally, Peter perceived that God is not sectarian.

Then Peter opened his mouth, and said, Of a truth I perceive that God is no respecter of persons: but in every nation he that feareth him, and worketh righteousness, is accepted with him (Acts 10:34, 35)

The Spirit may have known that after Peter had preached to the gentiles, he would not give an "altar call" for them to receive the baptism of the Holy Spirit. Therefore, He fell on them right in the middle of Peter's sermon.

While Peter yet spake these words, the Holy Ghost fell on them which heard the word (Acts 10:44).

My first experience among Catholic Charismatics was similar to Peter's. I made it through the singing, but when they began to say "Hail Mary" using rosary beads, I began to say to myself, "Unclean, unclean!"

47

Then followed a miraculous healing service with much praying in tongues. I perceived that God was not hung up on theology as I. And since He changes not, I must change.

Later, Paul rebuked Peter for his sectarian actions at Antioch. **But when Peter was come to Antioch, I withstood him to the face, because he was to be blamed. For before that certain came from James, he did eat with the Gentiles: but when they were come, he withdrew and separated himself, fearing them which were of the circumcision (Gal. 2:11, 12).**

Rising Above

As Velda and I were watching the news, we saw people pouring over the Berlin Wall. In that time of rejoicing, the Spirit seemed to speak these words: "Notice the wall is still standing and yet the people are free." Then he led me to compare sectarian walls to this wall. It is not necessary to pull down the walls; it is only necessary to break the authority of darkness and bondage so the people can rise above and go over the walls.

I wept and asked God's forgiveness for trying so hard to tear down walls all these years. He assured me that the wind of His Spirit would cause us to rise above all walls if we would only ask and stretch forth our wings in faith. The Song of Solomon speaks of this very thing. The Lord is speaking to His spouse—His sectarian Church.

A garden inclosed is my sister, my spouse; a spring shut up, a fountain sealed. Thy plants are an orchard of pomegranates, with pleasant fruits; camphire, with spikenard. Spikenard and saffron; calamus and cinnamon, with all trees of frankincense; myrrh and aloes, with all the chief

spices: A fountian of gardens, a well of living waters, and streams from Lebanon. Awake, O north wind; and come, thou south; blow upon my garden, that the spices thereof may flow out. Let my beloved come into his garden, and eat his pleasant fruits (S. Sol. 4:12-16).

I understand this scripture can be interpreted in more than one way. The garden inclosed could mean God's hedge of protection. But the place of safety can also become a wall in which everything is turned inward with no outward flow. When this happens, strong winds must come to blow us out of our "sectarian comfort zone."

If the wells of living waters and fragrance of the fruit of the Spirit are only in our circle, the only thing that will change it is the wind. It will toss things back and forth awhile.

Winds Of The Holy Spirit

Sometimes we invite a gentle south breeze to blow on our walled garden, but never let a "blue norther" follow that. The Holy Spirit may come in the form of the "winds of adversity." God's purpose cannot be seen if a sectarian spirit is in control because this spirit is very self-centered. The group becomes a "Bless Me Club."

I believe God gives and takes away. He purges out things which are not needed. Sometimes, Christians hoard the spiritual fruits and gifts. The fan of the Holy Spirit blows away what is no longer needed.

I indeed baptize you with water unto repentance: but he that cometh after me is mightier than I, whose shoes I am not worthy to bear: he shall baptize you with the Holy Ghost, and with fire: whose fan is in his hand, and he will throughly purge his floor, and gather his wheat into the

garner; but he will burn up the chaff with unquenchable fire (Matt. 3:11, 12).

The chaff protects the grain until it comes to maturity. It serves a vital purpose in the infancy stage, but must be released for the breaking process to begin. We must earnestly cry out for the winds to come. There will be temporary discomfort, but resurrection power will follow.

Why does it take so long to enter into a fruitful ministry? we ask. May I ask you a question? Will you receive a sudden mighty rushing wind as they did on the day of Pentecost? Usually we want to wait for a convenient season—when the children are out of school, our debts are paid or the money is flowing. Will you be moved by a source you can't fully and rationally explain? If the answer is a hearty "YES", then you may be launched quickly.

And suddenly there came a sound from heaven as of a rushing mighty wind, and it filled all the house where they were sitting (Acts 2:2).

The wind bloweth where it listeth, and thou hearest the sound thereof, but canst not tell whence it cometh, and whither it goeth: so is everyone that is born of the Spirit (Jn. 3:8).

God promised Paul—through an angel—that he would go to Rome. Little did he know the type of transportation God had booked for him. He went to Rome as a prisoner on a ship, tossed by storms all the way. One might ask why he did not just rebuke the storm like Jesus did. He probably tried, but it didn't work. Why? Could he not find anyone to "agree as touching anything" with him? The answer is that God's higher purpose was being carrried out.

Devilish winds can look the same to the natural eye as the wind of the Holy Spirit. Discernment comes only through daily brokenness before God and warfaring with high praises and the two-edged sword. Many are looking for a formula or a "pat answer", but there is no substitute for daily inviting Jesus, through praise and the Word, to inhabit our lives.

Paul warned the crew that the voyage would end in disaster. That is exactly what happened. The ship was destroyed, but 276 lives were spared. He would have been accused of making a faithless, negative confession by some of our day.

In this day we will see many sectarian "ships" (man-made institutions) destroyed which once served a purpose but are no longer needed. Like with Paul, there was a time to stay on board the ship, and a time to abandon it. On the island of Melita they had a miraculous evangelistic crusade with signs, wonders and miracles. I wonder if the island people had invited other evangelists to come and they insisted on traveling "first class". Paul's team was ready for ministry. Their hearts had been knit together by going through adversity. They had even learned to pray and fast together (see Acts 27, 28).

Bring All Your Friends, Lord

As Christians, first of all we must invite Jesus inside our garden walls. Then He invites all His friends—some of whom may not meet our approval. But since they are accepted by the Father through the blood of His Son, Jesus, let's be gracious to His friends.

I am come into my garden, my sister, my spouse: I have gathered my myrrh with my spice; I have eaten my honeycomb with my honey; I have drunk my wine with my milk: eat, O friends; drink, yea, drink abundantly, O beloved (S. Sol. 5:1).

Chapter Five

SPIRIT OF LAWLESSNESS
(PIRAM, KING OF JARMUTH)

The next enemy king is *Piram*, which in Hebrew means "running wildly, as a wild ass." My interpretation of this name is the ruler spirit of lawlessness. This spirit is the opposite of legalism. The nature of devils is to take truth to the extreme and pervert it. The growth process of a believer can be compared to the pendulum of a clock, swinging back and forth. When the pendulum swings, a wrong spirit can take hold of that pendulum and try to keep it from returning to safe middle ground.

In Romans Paul expresses the great and wonderful truth that Christ died for sinners.

"But God commendeth his love toward us, in that, while we were yet sinners, Christ died for us" (Rom. 5:8). The balance is found in the next chapter: **"What shall we say then? Shall we continue in sin, that grace may abound? God forbid. How shall we, that are dead to sin, live any longer therein?"** (Rom. 6:1–2).

God's Longsuffering Does Not Indicate Approval

Because of God's great grace, He tolerates sin for a season and continues to anoint and bless. Christians often mistake God's longsuffering for His "stamp of approval." This is not the case. If man continues to sin long enough, it will surely be brought to light. God is sovereign. He chooses when to reveal sin; it may be the first offense or the fiftieth.

During the days of the great tent revivals, thousands of documented miracles were worked through many men and women. However, many of these same men and women's lives and ministries ended tragically because of a spirit of lawlessness. This has propagated a distrust in healing ministries today.

In ministers these days, the fear of God, integrity and a right spirit are too often missing. For a time, the anointing remains, due to the longsuffering of our sovereign God. But I have great hope, because I believe the pendulum is swinging away from lawlessness.

Eternal Security Through Active Faith

Many of us grew up under legalism concerning salvation. One did not know for sure that he was saved until he walked through the "Pearly Gates." When my wife and I received the baptism of the Holy Spirit, the revelation of "saved by grace through faith" came to us. But we didn't know that faith without works is dead (see James. 2:17). The theology of "once saved, always saved" sounded good, but we noticed that people continually practicing things such as adultry would use this theology as license to habitually sin.

53

The Boundary Of The Spirit

There is still a boundry for belivers. It is "the law of the spirit" and "the law of liberty". True, we have been redeemed from the curse of the letter of the law which kills. We are now subject to a law not written on tablets of stone or in a book, but in our minds and hearts.

For this is the covenant that I will make with the house of Israel after those days, saith the Lord; I will put my laws into their mind, and write them in their hearts: and I will be to them a God, and they shall be to me a people: and they shall not teach every man his neighbour, and every man his brother, saying, Know the Lord: for all shall know me, from the least to the greatest (Heb. 8:10, 11).

Let me make it clear at this point that now most of my guidance comes from reading the Bible. But I read the Bible for many years and it was just a history book which scared and condemned me. The Spirit of Truth operating in my life made the great differance.

There is therefore now no condemnation to them which are in Christ Jesus, who walk not after the flesh, but after the Spirit. For the law of the Spirit of life in Christ Jesus hath made me free from the law of sin and death (Rom. 8:1, 2).

Freedom from the law of sin and death must be walked out in obedient faith, as the Lord leads us.

Spiritual Rock Of Revelation

The rock upon which God wrote the commandments that He gave to Moses was a type of the spiritual rock on which we rely today. This rock is a knowing in the heart and mind; it is a sure foundation on which one can walk and build. Hebrews 11:1 calls it "substance." The water Jesus walked on was not substance according to natural facts, but in the spiritual realm it was.

Matthew 7:13-27 Summarizes what we have just covered:

Enter ye in at the strait gate: for wide is the gate, and broad is the way, that leadeth to destruction, and many there be which go in thereat: because strait is the gate, and narrow is the way, which leadeth unto life, and few there be that find it. Beware of false prophets, which come to you in sheep's clothing, but inwardly they are ravening wolves. Ye shall know them by their fruits. Do men gather grapes of thorns, or figs of thistles? Even so every good tree bringeth forth good fruit; but a corrupt tree bringeth forth evil fruit. A good tree cannot bring forth evil fruit, neither can a corrupt tree bring forth good fruit. Every tree that bringeth not forth good fruit is hewn down, and cast into the fire. Wherefore by their fruits ye shall know them. Not every one that saith unto me, Lord, Lord, shall enter into the kingdom of heaven; but he that doeth the will of my Father which is in heaven. Many will say to me in that day, Lord, Lord, have we not prophesied in thy name? and in thy name have cast out devils? and in thy name done many wonderful works? And then will I profess unto them, I never knew you: depart from me, ye that work iniquity. Therefore whosoever heareth these sayings of mine, and doeth them, I will liken him to a wise man, which built his house upon a rock: and the rain descended, and the floods came, and the winds blew, and beat upon that house; and it fell not: for it was founded upon a rock. And every one that heareth these sayings of mine, and doeth them not, shall be likened unto a foolish man, which built his

house upon the sand: and the rain deceded, and the floods came, and the winds blew, and beat upon the house; and it fell and great was the fall of it.

Notice the word iniquity in verse 23. It is better translated in the New American Standard version as "lawlessness".

"And then I will declare to them, 'I never knew you; DEPART FROM ME, YOU WHO PRACTICE LAWLESSNESS'" (Matt. 7:23 NAS).

The content of this portion of scripture admonishes us to beware of false prophets whose fruit is dead. These false prophets say that there are no boundries for Christians. The truth is, the way to life is not broad, but narrow; it will require some searching to find it. Many will fail to seek truth and act in self-will—even some who have experienced the flow of the gifts of the Holy Spirit.

Many assume that Jesus is talking about those who have never experienced redemption from sin when he says, "I never Knew you". But the meaning of the word *knew* means "to have intercourse, whereby seed is conceived and a child is born." It is the same word used here:

And Adam knew Eve his wife; and she conceived, and bare Cain, and said, I have gotten a man from the Lord (Gen. 4:1).

In Matthew 7:23 (above) Jesus is referring to those who have never entered into a covenant relationship with Him. He is talking about those who have never allowed spiritual intercourse, and therefore have born no spiritual fruit. Pretty words are useless; in the end we will be known by our spiritual fruit, not by what we said. True fruit glorifies the Father God. It is possible to use the gifts of the Holy Spirit to glorify self and build one's own kingdom, and not the kingdom of God. This is the spirit of lawlessness.

Law Of Liberty, Love And Spirit

Stand fast therefore in the liberty wherewith Christ hath made us free, and be not entangled again with the yoke of bondage (Gal. 5:1).

For, brethren, ye have been called unto liberty; only use not liberty for an occassion to the flesh, but by love serve one another. For all the law is fulfilled in one word, even in this; thou shalt love thy neighbor as thyself. But if ye bite and devour one another, take heed that ye be not consumed one of another. This I say then, Walk in the Spirit, and ye shall not fulfill the lust of the flesh. For the flesh lusteth against the Spirit, and the Spirit against the flesh: and these are contrary the one to the other: so that ye cannot do the things that ye would. But if ye be led of the Spirit, ye are not under the law (Gal. 5:13-18).

Wrong Spirit of Agreement

Ananias and Sapphira (Acts 5) are New Testament examples of Christians controlled by a spirit of lawlessness. They were free to do anything they wished with their money, but they were judged because they lied to the Holy Ghost. This is a case where two were in agreement, but the thing they agreed upon was not the revealed will of God.

But a certain man named Ananias, with Sapphira his wife, sold a possession, and kept back part of the price, his wife also being privy to it, and brought a certain part, and laid it at the apostles' feet. But Peter said, Ananias, why hath Satan filled thine heart to lie to the Holy Ghost, and to keep back part of the price of the land? Whiles it remained, was it not thine own? and after it was

sold, was it not in thine own power? why hast thou conceived this thing in thine heart? thou has not lied unto men, but unto God. And Ananias hearing these words fell down, and gave up the ghost: and great fear came on all of them that heard these things (Acts 5:1-5).

Again I say unto you, That if two of you shall agree on earth as touching any thing that they shall ask, it shall be done for them of my Father which is in heaven. For where two or three are gathered together in my name, there am I in the midst of them (Matt. 18:19, 20).

This passage has been used many times in a lawless way. The key to understanding these verses is knowing that "gathered together in my name" means "in accordance with my spirit-revealed will." When the Spirit draws two people together, their requests are not based on the wants and desires of two natural minds, but on the mind of Christ. This is the basis of covenant relationship. The Lord Jesus Christ, the Living Word, is the mediator.

Being ruled by a spirit of lawlessness results in a lack of the fear of the Lord.

The fear of the Lord is the beginning of knowledge: but fools despise wisdom and instruction (Prov. 1:7)

Purging Up Front

Notice the cycle of events in Acts 5:

And great fear came upon all the church, and upon as many as heard these things. And by the hands of the apostles were many signs and wonders wrought among the people; (and they were all with one accord in Solomon's porch. And of the rest durst no man join himself to them: but the people

58

magnified them. And believers were the more added to the Lord, multitudes both of men and women) (Acts 5:11-14).

The order we see here is:
1. Purging of the spirit of lawlessness.
2. Fear of the Lord.
3. Signs and wonders.
4. One accord.
5. Respect for God's authority working through apostles.
6. Numbers multiplied.

Today, the order is still the same. But many leaders will not purge out persons who are givers of money, even if they are liars and deceivers. Purging only comes when we, the body of Christ, ask for it.

For by fire and by his sword will the Lord plead with all flesh: and the slain of the Lord shall be many (Is. 66:16).

And fear not them which kill the body, but are not able to kill the soul: but rather fear him which is able to destroy both soul and body in hell (Matt. 10:28).

The Holy "Spot Remover"

The purging taking place today in the Church is a sign of the times. Jesus is coming for a Church without spot or wrinkle.

That he might sanctify and cleanse it with the washing of water by the word, that he might present it to himself a glorious church, not having spot, or wrinkle, or any such thing: but that it should be holy and without blemish (Eph. 5:26-27).

The Word tells us what it means to be unspotted:

But whoso looketh into the perfect law of liberty, and continueth therein, he being not a

59

forgetful hearer, but a doer of the work, this man shall be blessed in his deed. If any man among you seem to be religious, and bridleth not his tongue, but deceiveth his own heart, this man's religion is vain. Pure religion and undefiled before God and the Father is this, To visit the fatherless and widows in their affliction, and to keep himself unspotted from the world (James 1:25-27).

Jude described lawlessness as spots in one's love feast.

For there are certain men crept in unawares, who were before of old ordained to this condemnation, ungodly men, turning the grace of our God into lasciviousness, and denying the only Lord God, and our Lord Jesus Christ. I will therefore put you in remembrance, though ye once knew this, how that the Lord, having saved the people out of the land of Egypt, afterward destroyed them that believed not. And the angels which kept not their first estate, but left their own habitation, he hath reserved in everlasting chains under darkness unto the judgment of the great day. Even as Sodom and Gomorrha, and the cities about them in like manner, giving themselves over to fornication, and going after strange flesh, are set forth for an example, suffering the vengeance of eternal fire. Likewise also these filty dreamers defile the flesh, despise dominion, and speak evil of dignities. Yet Michael the archangel, when contending with the devil he disputed about the body of Moses, durst not bring against him a railing accusation, but said, The Lord rebuke thee. But these speak evil of those things which they know not: but what they know naturally, as brute beasts, in those things they corrupt themselves. Woe unto them! for they have gone in the way of Cain, and ran greedily after the

error of Balaam for reward, and perished in the gainsaying of Core. These are spots in your feasts of charity, when they feast with you, feeding themselves without fear: clouds they are without water, carried about of winds; trees whose fruit withereth, without fruit, twice dead, plucked up by the roots; raging waves of the sea, foaming out their own shame; wandering stars, to whom is reserved the blackness of darkness for ever (Jude 4-13).

It is hard to misunderstand the book of Jude. It is so clear. It was written as a warning to believers who have rebelled against God's authority and fallen away, using grace as an excuse for willful and habitual sin.

The Old Testament gives examples of how God feels about this. Today He feels the same; He never changes. Even the angels who have left their first estate are condemned to hell. The words *brute beasts* refer to the antichrist beast, which will rule in the world for a season. His nature is anger, murder, greed and service for reward rather than love.

Notice these words in verse 12: "spots in your feasts of charity." They were always taking and never giving, no fear of God, no fruit, twice dead, no depth in the Word. "Twice dead" indicates one who has been delivered from spiritual death and fallen back into that state again.

The alarming thing is that people who are ruled by religious spirits continue to go through the motions of Christianity. They do not discern their state nor do most of their brethren.

Religious Adrenaline is a Counterfeit Flow

Samson is another Old Testament example of danger—going through the motions without realizing that the power of the Holy Spirit is missing.

61

And she said, The Philistines be upon thee, Samson. And he awoke out of his sleep, and said, I will go out as at other times before, and shake myself. And he wist not that the Lord was departed from him (Judg. 16:20).

Often after the Pentecostal power is gone, the religious spirit of Pentecostal shakings remain.

These be they who separate themselves, sensual, having not the Spirit. But ye, beloved, building up yourselves on your most holy faith, praying in the Holy Ghost (Jude 19-20).

The word *sensual* refers to the beastly, rational mind. They once built their faith through praying in unknown tongues, but departed from that practice. It is not a sin to never have spoken in tongues, but, it would be a sin not to use this gift after receiving it.

Chapter Six

SPIRIT OF RATIONALISM
(JAPHIA, KING OF LACHISH)

The enemy king Japhia is *yapha* in Hebrew. It means "to shine, show self, be light." Since he was a type of an enemy spirit, by this description we know he must represent an angel of light called rationalism.

And no marvel; for Satan himself is transformed into an angel of light. Therefore it is no great thing if his ministers also be transformed as the ministers of righteousness; whose end shall be according to their works (2 Cor. 11:14–15).

The spirit of rationalism hinders true faith, which operates by a higher law than natural fact. Rationalism does not allow faith to arise unless the natural mind has complete understanding. The rational mind becomes its own god, taking the high place of authority. The human mind is a beautiful servant, but a very poor master.

Paul wrote to Timothy that this would be a big problem in the last days.

Traitors, heady, highminded, lovers of pleasures more than lovers of God; having a form of

63

godliness, but denying the power thereof: from such turn away. For of this sort are they which creep into houses, and lead captive silly women laden with sins, led away with divers lusts, ever learning, and never able to come to the knowledge of the truth (2 Tim. 3:4–7).

The Greek meaning of *heady* is "rash and headstrong." *Highminded* means "to envelop with smoke, inflate with self-conceit, be lifted up with pride." This was the first thing Adam and Eve did after eating from the tree of the knowledge of good and evil. The fig-leaf apron was a cover-up designed by the natural mind to conceal fear and guilt.

Second Timothy 3:5 tells us that this spirit is religious but refuses to allow the Spirit of power to function. Satan will try to take the God-given gifts we possess and pervert them for his purposes—unless we use spiritual weapons to pull down the reasonings of the mind.

For the weapons of our warfare are not carnal, but mighty through God to the pulling down of strong holds; casting down imaginations, and every high thing that exalteth itself against the knowledge of God, and bringing into captivity every thought to the obedience of Christ (2 Cor. 10:4–5).

This I say therefore, and testify in the Lord, that ye henceforth walk not as other Gentiles walk, in the vanity of their mind (Eph. 4:17).

The word vanity is *maten* in Greek. It means "empty manipulations; unsuccessful search."

Rational Fact or Truth

Many times there is confusion between natural fact and truth. Jesus defined truth in this way:

Sanctify them through thy truth: thy word is truth (John 17:17).

Faith must be based on what is unseen. The natural mind says, "Seeing is believing." The Word says, "Believe and you shall see."

Now faith is the substance of things hoped for, the evidence of things not seen. For by it the elders obtained a good report. Through faith we understand that the worlds were framed by the word of God, so that things which are seen were not made of things which do appear (Heb. 11:1–3).

Consider the account of Jesus raising Lazarus from the dead: Jesus saith unto her, Said I not unto thee that, if thou wouldest believe, thou shouldest see the glory of God? (John 11:40).

When Jesus was first told that His friend Lazarus was sick, He spoke words of truth. When Jesus heard that, he said, This sickness is not unto death, but for the glory of God, that the Son of God might be glorified thereby (John 11:4).

Remember, when Jesus Christ, the Living Word speaks, He overrules all natural laws—including those governing medical science. God's nature is to speak things which are not as if they are.

(As it is written, I have made thee a father of many nations,) before him whom he believed, even God, who quickeneth the dead, and calleth those things which be not as though they were (Rom. 4:17).

Jesus had a choice to make. I'm sure His emotions were urging Him to quickly take action on the natural fact of the matter. But His spirit was saying to pray two days, lest He walk in the darkness of natural fact instead of the light of truth.

Our friend Lazarus sleepeth; but I go, that I may awake him out of sleep. Then said his disciples, Lord, if he sleep, he shall do well. Howbeit Jesus spake of his death: but they thought that he had

spoken of taking of rest in sleep. Then said Jesus unto them plainly, Lazarus is dead (John 11:11–14).

Here Jesus spoke both the fact of the matter and the truth of the matter—fact, he is dead; truth, he only sleeps, and I will raise him.

Tongues go Beyond the Rational

I am convinced that during this time Jesus was praying beyond His understanding in an unknown tongue of the Holy Spirit. To me, it is quite evident because the words *groaning in the spirit* are used here in the same way as in Romans 8 concerning praying in the Spirit.

Likewise the Spirit also helpeth our infirmities: for we know not what we should pray for as we ought: but the Spirit itself maketh intercession for us with groanings which cannot be uttered. And he that searcheth the hearts knoweth what is the mind of the Spirit, because he maketh intercession for the saints according to the will of God (Rom. 8:26–27).

When Jesus therefore saw her weeping, and the Jews also weeping which came with her, he groaned in the spirit, and was troubled (John 11:33).

This particular word *troubled* means "to stir the water." Timothy was commanded by Paul to stir up the gift of faith, a gift that was also in his mother and grandmother. I believe Jesus was stirring up this same gift through praying in tongues.

Wherefore I put thee in remembrance that thou stir up the gift of God, which is in thee by the putting on of my hands (2 Tim. 1:6).

Jesus therefore again groaning in himself cometh to the grave (John 11:38).

Praying in tongues moves me from the natural mind to the mind of Christ. When Jesus wept, I believe

His tears were not of sorrow, but a manifestation of the anointing of the Spirit.

Rationalistic Spirits Violently Oppose Truth

Religious spirits are violent and often are at the root of murder. The religious Pharisees were controlled by a rationalistic spirit driving them to try to kill Him rather than believe the miracle of Lazarus' resurrection..

Then from that day forth they took counsel together for to put him to death (John 11:53).

Acknowledging Fact Does Not Hinder Faith

Twelve spies were sent to search out Canaan, and were commanded to obtain the facts. When they returned, the vote was ten for walking by fact and two for walking in faith by the light of truth.

And Caleb stilled the people before Moses, and said, Let us go up at once, and possess it; for we are well able to overcome it. But the men that went up with him said, We be not able to go up against the people; for they are stronger than we (Num. 13:30–31).

Caleb was not controlled by a spirit of rationalism. He followed the Lord fully, even beyond his natural understanding.

But my servant Caleb, because he had another spirit with him, and hath followed me fully, him will I bring into the land whereinto he went; and his seed shall possess it (Num. 14:24).

Knowing natural facts does not hinder faith as long as we are not bound by them. Sometimes we, as people of faith, are accused of not facing the facts of life. That charge is justified at times, I am sure. The cultist belief of "mind over matter" does not accept facts.

Once a man of the Christian Science belief was saved in a church where I pastored. His questions of how positive confession—which we were practicing at the time—was different from what he had been taught were hard to answer. Fervent prayer on the matter revealed what I am sharing.

On another occasion, ten of us were going on a thirty-day foreign mission trip. The leader said, "We have plenty of money for food when we arrive." Later I found out this was only a positive confession. I always ask for facts now.

Technicalities Overlooked

Wording our prayers incorrectly does not hinder answers from coming. Joshua did not understand the technical scientific facts that the earth revolves instead of the sun and moon when he commanded them to stand still. God heard and answered him because of his faith. Faith is of the heart, and not of the mind. (see Josh. 10:12)

Above All We Can Ask Or Think

God is able to do beyond all we can ask or think if we will let His power work in us. This happens when we pray in unknown tongues, beyond our understanding, as we have mentioned before.

Now unto him that is able to do exceeding abundantly above all that we ask or think, according to the power that worketh in us, unto him be the glory in the church by Jesus Christ throughout all ages, world without end. (Eph. 3:20–21).

But God hath chosen the foolish things of the

world to confound the wise; and God hath chosen the weak things of the world to confound the things which are mighty; and base things of the world, and things which are despised, hath God chosen, yea, and things which are not, to bring to nought things that are: that no flesh should glory in his presence (1 Cor. 1:27-29).

May the God of all grace keep our hearts and minds, and use us in a way that brings maximum glory to Himself. Amen!

Chapter Seven

SPIRIT OF RITUALISM
(DEBIR, KING OF EGLON)

S ome of the meanings for the name *Debir* are "to shorten: the shrine, or innermost part of the sanctuary; to arrange words to speak, to rehearse." To me, this speaks of a ritualistic spirit. The desire of lukewarm, carnal Christians seems to be short worship services with no surprises. They want the leader to initiate all activity and the congregation to be spectators. They do not like spontaneity; everything must be thoroughly rehearsed. For many, the building is a sanctuary and a shrine and becomes an object of worship.

Moses was told by God to make a brazen serpent for the healing of the children of Israel. However, later the people began to worship the image itself, so God had it destroyed.

He removed the high places, and brake the images, and cut down the groves, and brake in pieces the brasen serpent that Moses had made: for unto those days the children of Israel did burn incense to it: and he called it Nehushtan (2 Kings 18:4).

70

It would not surprise me if our Lord does not do the same thing with some of the extremely extravagant religious structures of our day.

What? know ye not that your body is the temple of the Holy Ghost which is in you, which ye have of God, and ye are not your own? For ye are bought with a price: therefore glorify God in your body, and in your spirit, which are God's (1 Cor. 6:19–20).

The Enemy's Purpose is to Bind the Flow

A ritualistic spirit allows no flow of the anointing. This spirit does not stop people from receiving the Holy Spirit but reduces everything to man's ability to perform—being governed by the clock.

What may be surprising is, this happens in so-called Spirit-filled churches. The ritual has simply changed. Perhaps the same people give the message in tongues each week, with the same one giving the interpretation. The congregation waits for the praise leader to sing in tongues, then follows on cue. The same people go to the altar every service for prayer. Members go home unchanged.

Musicians and singers are particularly susceptible to this spirit. Any suggested change is protested in different ways—from pouting to turning the volume up and violently pounding the strings of their instrument. If they have rehearsed three songs and are asked to sing only one of them, they will pick a medley that includes parts of six songs. As a musician, I speak from experience.

During worship, we go from one extreme of time to the other—from very short to very long. There are no shortcuts in the presence of God, neither do we get there by extending our time of seeking.

In the wilderness tabernacle, several steps were required in order to move from the outer courtyard to the most holy place. We try to encourage every person to pray before coming together. There should be no preconceived idea about how and when the Holy Spirit will manifest Himself. Yet, we can be confident He will show up each time. Of course, the leaders should have a general plan, but they should always be sensitive to change in the direction the Holy Spirit is flowing.

Many times I will preach first, then move from there into praise and the rest of the service. I do not always know why at first, but afterward is it usually apparent why it was God's order for the day.

On other occasions a praise team will give a call for salvation and healing before I preach. There was a time when we could not do this type of thing. We had to grow into it, learning to respect the anointing in each individual, knowing the heart of every leader.

Ritual or Good Habit?

In the early days of learning it seemed Wednesday night services were a ritual, so I changed to Thursday nights. There was one thing wrong—only a small number came. I remember praying and fasting that the Lord would rebuke the people for their rebellion. Instead, the Lord rebuked *me* for calling good habits "rituals". Upon returning to Wednesdays, the numbers returned to normal.

It is evident that Peter and John had a habit of praying every day at the ninth hour (see Acts 3:1). Again, we need to discern between what is ritual and what is a good habit. We can train the natural man for good or for evil.

72

Stephen Killed by Ritualistic Spirits

And they stirred up the people, and the elders, and the scribes, and came upon him, and caught him, and brought him to the council, and set up false witnesses, which said, This man ceaseth not to speak blasphemous words against this holy place, and the law: for we have heard him say, that this Jesus of Nazareth shall destroy this place, and shall change the customs which Moses delivered us (Acts 6:12–14).

The root of Stephen's murder was a religious spirit. The people were angry because the Holy Spirit was moving strongly through Stephen to change the customs of Moses. Their eyes and ears were hindered by this ritualistic spirit so they could not receive the blessings of the Good News of Jesus Christ.

But Solomon built him an house. Howbeit the most High dwelleth not in temples made with hands; as saith the prophet, Heaven is my throne, and earth is my footstool: what house will ye build me? saith the Lord: or what is the place of my rest? Hath not my hand made all these things? Ye stiffnecked and uncircumcised in heart and ears, ye do always resist the Holy Ghost: as your fathers did, so do ye (Acts 7:47–51).

If you have seen demon-possessed people you will recognize the description in the following verses:

When they heard these things, they were cut to the heart, and they gnashed on him with their teeth (Acts 7:54).

Then they cried out with a loud voice, and stopped their ears, and ran upon him with one accord, and cast him out of the city, and stoned him: and the witnesses laid down their clothes at a young man's feet, whose name was Saul (Acts 7:57–58).

Glory Heralds Change

According to Acts 6:15, the glory of God upon Stephen was so strong that his face looked like that of an angel. This brings us to a general principle: the manifestation of the glory of God always heralds change.

When people are bound by a ritualistic spirit, they resist any demonstration of the glory of God and usually don't realize why they are driven to act in such a way. It is important that intercessors understand that when anger and violence erupts within a church or family, the spirit to bind is not always the obvious one. But any spirit can be discerned and bound with a solid rock word of the Holy Spirit.

Often, when praying for family members or friends, they will become very agitated. The reason is that the Holy Spirit is suggesting a change of lifestyle, and the ritualistic spirit is screaming "No!" God is revealing Himself to this person as the Lord of Glory, and he sees the contrast with his own life. If those praying will continue to worship and rejoice in Spirit and in truth, this anger will soon turn to repentance.

But we all, with open face beholding as in a glass the glory of the Lord, are changed into the same image from glory to glory, even as by the Spirit of the Lord (2 Cor. 3:18).

An Old Testament type of this is found in the book of Exodus.

And Moses was not able to enter into the tent of the congregation, because the cloud abode thereon, and the glory of the Lord filled the tabernacle. And when the cloud was taken up from over the tabernacle, the children of Israel went onward in all their journeys (Ex. 40:35–36).

We must overcome the fear of the unknown. When

the glory cloud begins to move, our great **Provider** brings us out from one kind of security into something much better. Sometimes a wilderness of confusion lies between.

I am the Lord your God, which brought you forth out of the land of Egypt, to give you the land of Canaan, and to be your God (Lev. 25:38).

And he brought us out from thence, that he might bring us in, to give us the land which he sware unto our fathers (Deut. 6:23).

Adam, Eve, Job and Jonah

Religious spirits like darkness and will resist a face-to-face encounter with the presence of God. To me, the words *glory* and *presence of God* mean the same thing. Adam and Eve, Job and Jonah all shared this common fear, as we can see in the following verses:

And they heard the voice of the Lord God walking in the garden in the cool of the day: and Adam and his wife hid themselves from the presence of the Lord God amongst the trees of the garden (Gen. 3:8).

Therefore am I troubled at his presence: when I consider, I am afraid of him. For God maketh my heart soft, and the Almighty troubleth me (Job 23:15–16).

But Jonah rose up to flee unto Tarshish from the presence of the Lord, and went down to Joppa; and he found a ship going to Tarshish: so he paid the fare thereof, and went down into it, to go with them unto Tarshish from the presence of the Lord (Jonah 1:3).

Deliverance Rituals, without Revelation

During the seventies, we became experienced in

casting out devils. In our newness, the Lord blessed a certain ritual that we had learned from others. When He was ready for us to move to a more mature way, the ritual ceased to work. That was a confusing time. We thought this was an original formula until it was pointed out that it stemmed from a sixteenth-century Roman Catholic book on exorcism. This was one reason why the seven sons of Sceva were unsuccessful in casting out devils.

Then certain of the vagabond Jews, exorcists, took upon them to call over them which had evil spirits the name of the Lord Jesus, saying, We adjure you by Jesus whom Paul preacheth (Acts 19:13).

First of all, they took it upon themselves, as opposed to being led; secondly, they had no personal revelation and were only acting on a word which they had heard preached by Paul.

This is very typical of how religious spirits act today. Ministers sometimes even use the same voice and mannerisms of their favorite preachers. That's one reason why they are often overpowered by demons and we come away from a service unchallenged and unchanged.

Ritualism Bound by the Glory

I'm longing for the day when the Church will no longer need men or women to lead them into worship. I look forward to a time when there will be such unity in worship that the preachers, priests and song leaders will all be "slain in the spirit" as in 2 Chronicles 5. This may be the only way the Lord can stop us from leading rituals.

It came even to pass, as the trumpeters and singers were as one, to make one sound to be heard

in praising and thanking the Lord; and when they lifted up their voice with the trumpets and cymbals and instruments of musick, and praised the Lord, saying, For he is good; for his mercy endureth forever; that then the house was filled with a cloud, even the house of the Lord; So that the priests could not stand to minister by reason of the cloud: for the glory of the Lord had filled the house of God (2 Chron. 5:13–14).

God's Cycle—shakings, Abundance, Peace

The shaking of this hour is designed to move the Church from things that can be shaken—such as rituals—to the riches of the unshakable kingdom of God.

For thus saith the Lord of hosts; Yet once, it is a little while, and I will shake the heavens, and the earth, and the sea, and the dry land; and I will shake all nations, and the desire of all nations shall come: and I will fill this house with glory, saith the Lord of hosts. The silver is mine, and the gold is mine, saith the Lord of hosts. The glory of this latter house shall be greater than of the former, saith the Lord of hosts: and in this place will I give peace, saith the Lord of hosts (Hag. 2:6–9).

Though we are in the midst of shakings greater than ever before—wars, earthquakes, political instability and famine—we must believe that it is only a sign that the glory of God will be manifested in greater measure also. The wealth of the world—silver, gold and oil—is being shaken into the kingdom of God, where it belonged all along. Peace will follow, such as the world has never known. We will learn to know Him as the Lord of hosts, the covenant God. He blesses the righteous in innumerable ways, as the sand

77

of the seashore and the stars of the sky.

And I will give thee the treasures of darkness, and hidden riches of secret places, that thou mayest know that I, the Lord, which call thee by thy name, am the God of Israel (Is. 45:3).

In the book of Hebrews we see that these events are still coming. Let us Rejoice!

Whose voice then shook the earth: but now he hath promised, saying, Yet once more I shake not the earth only, but also heaven. And this word, Yet once more, signifieth the removing of those things that are shaken, as of things that are made, that those things which cannot be shaken may remain. Wherefore we receiving a kingdom which cannot be moved, let us have grace, whereby we may serve God acceptably with reverence and godly fear: for our God is a consuming fire (Heb. 12:26–29).

It may be shocking to see true Christianity, once all the rituals are shaken out. But Christianity is a way of life rather than a place to perform or be entertained.

Chapter Eight

SPIRIT OF RELIGIOUS PRIDE
(AMORITE)

A ll five kings were of the Amorite tribe (see Joshua 10:5). Two words stand out in the Hebrew definition—publicity and prominence. My interpretation of *Amorite* is "religious pride." This chief of the ruler spirits drives men to build their own kingdoms.

Publicity

Present-day religious practice relies heavily upon billboards, television, radio, and newspapers for publicity instead of signs, wonders and miracles. Professionals are hired—many are not born again—to publicize the work of God in a carnal way.

And as the lame man which was healed held Peter and John, all the people ran together unto them in the porch that is called Solomon's, greatly wondering (Acts 3:11).

And by the hands of the apostles were many signs and wonders wrought among the people; (and they were all with one accord in Solomon's porch. And of the rest durst no man join himself to them:

but the people magnified them. And believers were
the more added to the Lord, multitudes both of men
and women.) Insomuch that they brought forth the
sick into the streets, and laid them on beds and
couches, that at the least the shadow of Peter
passing by might overshadow some of them. There
came also a multitude out of the cities round about
unto Jerusalem, bringing sick folks, and them
which were vexed with unclean spirits: and they
were healed every one (Acts 5:12–16).

Promotions used by man may generate great
numbers, but the promotion of the Holy Spirit moves
us into the innumerable.

And I will make thy seed as the dust of the
earth; so that if man can number the dust of the
earth, then shall thy seed also be numbered (Gen.
13:16).

Presently, I believe the Holy Spirit is grieved,
especially over America. Men have committed the
same sin as David when he numbered Israel and Judah.

And David's heart smote him after that he had
numbered the people. And David said unto the
Lord, I have sinned greatly in that I have done: and
now, I beseech thee, O Lord, take away the iniquity
of thy servant; for I have done very foolishly. . . . So
the Lord sent a pestilence upon Israel from the
morning even to the time appointed: and there died
of the people from Dan even to Beersheba seventy
thousand men (2 Sam. 24:10, 15).

Even though much light has been shed on divine
healing in our time, Christians continue to die of
pestilence or plagues such as cancer. This will continue
until true repentance of religious pride comes. Men
argue and point to an increase in the membership roll
or seating capacity of the "sanctuary" as evidence of
success. Only time and testing prove genuine success.

Prominence

When a pastor or priest is lifted to a place of prominence, many times, instead of assuming the role of servant, he becomes the star performer and the congregants are considered the ticket-paying (or tithe-paying) spectators. The paid musicians and supporting cast help him with the performance. This draws a crowd until someone across town puts on a better show. Then many "feel led" to change churches. It is no deep mystery. Show business is just that way.

During the sixties, I was a country music entertainer. My life's ambition had come to pass, and by some strange set of circumstances, I was included on road shows with Grand Ole Opry stars. What I thought would be glorious became a ten-year nightmare. So I recognize show business when I see it. It is a major enemy of true Christianity. The sad thing is that most Christians today do not discern the difference between natural charisma and the anointing of the Holy Spirit.

Lucifer, The Father Of Show-business Pride

Lucifer was cast out of heaven because he wanted to exalt himself as a star.

How art thou fallen from heaven, O Lucifer, son of the morning! how art thou cut down to the ground, which didst weaken the nations! For thou hast said in thine heart, I will ascend into heaven, I will exalt my throne above the stars of God: I will sit also upon the mount of the congregation, in the sides of the north: I will ascend above the heights of the clouds; I will be like the most High. Yet thou shalt be brought down to hell, to the sides of the pit (Is. 14:12–15).

81

The tempter who appeared to Eve in the Garden of Eden was the master spirit of showmanship. He was covered with precious stones, had an entire orchestra prepared in him, was an anointed angelic being and had much experience in the presence of God.

Thou hast been in Eden the garden of God; every precious stone was thy covering, the sardius, topaz, and the diamond, the beryl, the onyx, and the jasper, the sapphire, the emerald, and the carbuncle, and gold: the workmanship of thy tabrets and of thy pipes was prepared in thee in the day that thou wast created. Thou art the anointed cherub that covereth; and I have set thee so: thou wast upon the holy mountain of God; thou hast walked up and down in the midst of the stones of fire. Thou wast perfect in thy ways from the day that thou wast created, till iniquity was found in thee. By the multitude of thy merchandise they have filled the midst of thee with violence, and thou hast sinned: therefore I will cast thee as profane out of the mountain of God (Ezek. 28:13–16).

Where the real anointing is, there is always a counterfeit. It makes no sense to counterfeit a three-dollar bill. Lucifer's favorite place is not in a dead church, but where there is good worship and preaching—but little discernment.

In churches where men have not taken their places of leadership in the family and congregation, the door is open for the spirit of showmanship. Women are more easily moved by beautiful things. The color of the carpet and drapes can become so prominent that our places of worship often end up looking like theaters.

It is easy to get into the spirit of the music and leave Jesus out of our worship. It is easier to preach whatever receives the most audience approval rather than deliver the convicting Word of God. Without embracing a broken and contrite spirit daily, ministry becomes a performance.

It is essential that more attention be given to relationship with God than natural talents in selecting worship and ministry leaders.

Spirit-Directed Performance

Now let me try to balance this by referring to the production of Elijah and the prophets of Baal (see 1 Kings 18:25–39). This seemed a well-planned performance for the benefit of the spectators. Elijah played it for all it was worth—a drama filled with suspense and action with a fiery "grand finale." Of course, the Holy Spirit was directing the entire episode.

Sometimes we are guilty of misjudging a ministry. Often methods of evangelism are misjudged. The need may be to "hook" carnal-minded people on their level and bring them to the spiritual truth of Christ. But it is the Holy Spirit who directs such occasions.

And God wrought special miracles by the hands of Paul: so that from his body were brought unto the sick handkerchiefs of aprons, and the diseases departed from them, and the evil spirits went out of them (Acts 19:11–12).

And as we tarried there many days, there came down from Judaea a certain prophet, named Agabus. And when he was come unto us, he took Paul's girdle, and bound his own hands and feet, and said, Thus saith the Holy Ghost, So shall the Jews at Jerusalem bind the man that owneth this girdle, and shall deliver him into the hands of the Gentiles (Acts 21:10–11).

It is my conviction that "special performances"

must be directed by the Holy Spirit. The Church of Jesus Christ should never try to compete with worldly entertainment in order to draw a crowd or raise money.

Skillful Unto The Lord

Skillful performance in praise is pleasing to God as is plainly seen in the following scriptures:

Sing unto him a new song; play skilfully with a loud noise (Ps. 33:3).

And Chenaniah, chief of the Levites, was for song: he instructed about the song, because he was skilful (1 Chron. 15:22).

Like most things, praising the Lord depends on the thoughts and intentions of the heart, discernable only to the Spirit of God.

God resisteth the proud, but giveth grace unto the humble. Submit yourselves therefore to God. Resist the devil, and he will flee from you. Draw nigh to God, and he will draw nigh to you. Cleanse your hands, ye sinners; and purify your hearts, ye double minded (James 4:6–8).

For thus saith the high and lofty One that inhabiteth eternity, whose name is Holy; I dwell in the high and holy place, with him also that is of a contrite and humble spirit, to revive the spirit of the humble, and to revive the heart of the contrite ones (Is. 57:15).

For all those things hath mine hand made, and all those things have been, saith the Lord: but to this man will I look, even to him that is poor and of a contrite spirit, and trembleth at my word (Is. 66:2).

Power to resist the devil begins with humility before God, confessing our dependency on Jesus, who has destroyed all Satan's power. We overcome by faith. The grace (anointing) to bind, cast out and walk on the enemy is given to the humble.

Chapter Nine

HIGH PRAISE AND THE TWO-EDGED SWORD

Let the high praises of God be in their mouth, and a two-edged sword in their hand; to execute vengeance upon the heathen, and punishments upon the people; to bind their kings with chains, and their nobles with fetters of iron; to execute upon them the judgment written: this honour have all his saints. Praise ye the Lord (Ps. 149:6–9).

It is my belief that the kings and nobles mentioned here refer to spiritual enemies rather than political offices. Our warfare should not include speaking against men in high places but by speaking what has already been written against spiritual wickedness in high places.

At one time I considered spiritual warfare a difficult task, but now I know it is a joyful honor given to all God's saints. The key is unity of the Spirit. Our role as the corporate body of Christ is to execute what has been written. Let us be sure that we understand these mighty weapons.

A New Song

The command to sing a new song in the congregation is found in Psalm 149:1:

Praise ye the Lord. Sing unto the Lord a new song, and his praise in the congregation of saints.

This can be likened to the Day of Pentecost when the people were intoxicated with the "new wine" of the Holy Spirit. Nothing like this had ever happened before. They were worshipping beyond their natural understanding and ability.

Since singing a new song is something that is done in the congregation, fear of man must be overcome. With one's reputation on the line, it would be much more comfortable to sing a rehearsed, ritualistic song. But when a new song is sung, the fear of the Lord comes upon the entire assembly. Trusting God is the result.

And he hath put a new song in my mouth, even praise unto our God: many shall see it, and fear, and shall trust in the Lord (Ps. 40:3).

A new song is one never sung before; it does not come from the natural mind, but from the heart or spirit. The words flow the same way as spoken prophecy. When it is accompanied by an instrument, instead of the rational mind telling the fingers where to go next, the fingers follow the Spirit. All those participating are blessed by a skill beyond natural talents.

A singer's range is often wider under this anointing. In my experience, the song is never sung again; it is only for that special moment.

Sing unto him a new song; play skilfully with a loud noise (Ps. 33:3).

Skillful playing is not only supernatural; it comes from a commitment to practice. "Loudness" is tolerable only when the supernatural element is involved. With the anointing of the Spirit, a greater volume is not offensive to our ears. On the other hand, if a musician is playing loudly solely by natural talent, it can be very painful and distracting. It can result in the audience focusing on personalities instead of Jesus.

The Sacrifice Of Rejoicing

Let Israel rejoice in him that made him: let the children of Zion be joyful in their King (Ps. 149:2).

For we are the circumcision, which worship God in the spirit, and rejoice in Christ Jesus, and have no confidence in the flesh (Phil. 3:3).

This kind of rejoicing is celebrating our King and our new creation in Christ Jesus (see Eph. 4:24, 2 Cor. 5:17).

By him therefore let us offer the sacrifice of praise to God continually, that is, the fruit of our lips giving thanks to his name (Heb. 13:15).

Dance Your Pride Away

Let them praise his name in the dance: let them sing praises unto him with the timbrel and harp. For the Lord taketh pleasure in his people: he will beautify the meek with salvation (Ps. 149:3–4).

In the previous chapter, we saw religious pride as a strong spirit that must be bound. Sometimes we do not understand why we are to worship in dance. Dancing before the Lord breaks down pride in a person who has little natural talent. His feet must obey the Spirit instead of his natural mind. It is the same with the person who allows his fingers to follow the Spirit when prophesying on an instrument. During worship the Spirit wants our feet to dance, but the mind says, "I can't." We need to remember the scripture commands us to do it. So begin to be a "fool for Christ." Though it may not be pretty to others, the Lord takes pleasure in meekness and makes it a beautiful experience of deliverance from the bondage of religious pride.

The first time Velda and I went to a service and saw others dancing in the Spirit, we were shocked. Part of us wanted to run out while another part wanted to join in. We were standing near one of the most dignified, well-dressed men we had ever seen—extremely proper, with a three-piece suit and a well-trimmed mustache. Velda whispered to me, "If this man dances, I'll believe it's real." No sooner had she said the words than this man broke into a very fast jig, swinging his arms wildly. It only lasted about five seconds, then he resumed his very dignified posture as if nothing had happened. We said, "Okay, Lord, we'll do it *sometime*." It was quite awhile before we were free enough to yield to the Spirit in dance, but we never doubted from that day forward.

As with any Holy Spirit manifestation, there is also the fleshly, devilish counterfeit. There is no blessing in dancing for one who puts on a prideful show.

On Your Bed

Let the saints be joyful in glory: let them sing aloud upon their beds (Ps. 149:5).

This verse speaks to me of continual praise. Even when we awake early in the morning we can break forth into singing. The demons will say, "Oh no, that new creation is awake again," and they will flee like smoke on a windy day.

It could also apply to the bed of affliction. I have used praise as a weapon many times to bind sickness in myself, though I am sometimes slow to obey. I start out with a very feeble groan and stay with it until I gain strength to increase the volume. Soon the Spirit takes over and it is no longer a sacrifice, but joy. When this happens, my mind is no longer dwelling on the sickness, but on the Lord; I know that victory has come, no matter how I feel.

Worship Punishes Rulers Of Darkness

To execute vengeance upon the heathen, and punishments upon the people (Ps. 149:7).

High praise and the power of the Word punish the ruler spirits of darkness. It is the Lord's vengeance. True worship of God punishes Satan because his great desire is to have the saints worship him. Through worship he is bound with chains and his lesser nobles are shackled with iron.

We are accepted through the blood of Jesus. We rejoice because our names are written in Heaven. We say that Jesus has overcome and is seated in the high place of authority beside the Father, and by faith we are seated with Him. Jesus is vindicated from His unjust sentence upon the cross through the worship of the overcoming Church. Notice the connection between the anointing of the Holy Spirit and the vengeance of the Lord in the following scriptures.

The Spirit of the Lord God is upon me; because the Lord hath anointed me to preach good tidings unto the meek; he hath sent me to bind up the broken-hearted, to proclaim liberty to the captives, and the opening of the prison to them that are bound; to proclaim the acceptable year of the Lord, and the day of vengeance of our God; to comfort all that mourn; to appoint unto them that mourn in Zion, to give unto them beauty for ashes, the oil of joy for mourning, the garment of praise for the

spirit of heaviness; that they might be called **trees of righteousness, the planting of the Lord, that he might be glorified (Is. 61:1–3).**

We have an appointment with high praise on the mountain of Zion. As we keep this appointment, dead works give way to beauty; mourning yields to the oil of joy; and the spirit of heaviness is replaced by clothing from on high. This is worshipping "in spirit and in truth." In the account of Jesus and the woman at the well, Jesus was drawing this woman from religious talk into true worship.

Our fathers worshipped in this mountain; and ye say, that in Jerusalem is the place where men ought to worship. Jesus saith unto her, Woman, believe me, the hour cometh, when ye shall neither in this mountain, nor yet at Jerusalem, worship the Father. Ye worship ye know not what: we know what we worship: for salvation is of the Jews. But the hour cometh, and now is, when the true worshippers shall worship the Father in spirit and in truth: for the Father seeketh such to worship him. God is a Spirit: and they that worship him must worship him in spirit and in truth (John 4:20-24).

Worship need not occur in some geographical place, but in the Spirit. (The Old Testament type is Mount Zion.) Joshua commanded the Israelites to place stones upon the mouth of the cave, the hiding place of the enemy kings.

And Joshua said, Roll great stones upon the mouth of the cave, and set men by it for to keep them (Josh. 10:18).

See a parallel to these stones in 1 Peter 2:5–9:

Ye also, as lively stones, are built up a spiritual house, an holy priesthood, to offer up spiritual sacrifices, acceptable to God by Jesus Christ. Wherefore also it is contained in the scripture,

Behold, I lay in Sion a chief cornerstone, elect, precious: and he that believeth on him shall not be confounded. Unto you therefore which believe he is precious: but unto them which be disobedient, the stone which the builders disallowed, the same is made the head of the corner, and a stone of stumbling, a rock of offence, even to them which stumble at the word, being disobedient: whereunto also they were appointed. But ye are a chosen generation, a royal priesthood, an holy nation, a peculiar people; that ye should shew forth the praises of him who hath called you out of darkness into his marvellous light.

The context of this scripture is the sacrifice of praise. Praise is compared to the spiritual house of God, made up of precious stones that reflect light. The Foundation Stone is the source of all light. The smaller stones resting on this foundation are mirrors that collectively reflect marvelous light to the whole world. The result is that devils, having no darkness in which to hide, must flee. The Cornerstone is precious to believers but a rock of stumbling to the disobedient. It serves two purposes, just like the two-edged sword.

In the covenant between Jacob and Laban, the heap of stones was very important.

Now therefore come thou, let us make a covenant, I and thou, and let it be for a witness between me and thee. And Jacob took a stone, and set it up for a pillar. And Jacob said unto his brethren, Gather stones; and they took stones, and made an heap: and they did eat there upon the heap (Gen. 31:44–46).

The pillar of stone is a type for Christ, the Mediator or Head of the body. The smaller stones symbolize the individual members of the body, or house of God. Jesus mediates today through the body by shining His light on every matter concerning the Church. This is accomplished by Holy Spirit manifestations, working through each member. Sometimes we think this will happen with no effort on our part. However, notice it was the brethren who were responsible for gathering the stones.

The Two-Edged Sword

The two-edged sword purges or prunes so that we will bring forth more fruit. It also destroys spiritual wickedness in the midst of the Church.

Behold, I will make thee a new sharp threshing instrument having teeth: thou shalt thresh the mountains, and beat them small, and shalt make the hills as chaff. Thou shalt fan them, and the wind shall carry them away, and the whirlwind shall scatter them: and thou shalt rejoice in the Lord, and shalt glory in the Holy One of Israel (Is. 41:15–16).

Notice the tie between the sharp instrument—rejoicing in the Lord—and giving glory to God. This word is no respecter of persons. This word can cause numbers to decrease for a season,but in the long run the spiritual house will stand.

For the word of God is quick, and powerful, and sharper than any twoedged sword, piercing even to the dividing asunder of soul and spirit, and of the joints and marrow, and is a discerner of the thoughts and intents of the heart (Heb. 4:12).

The two-edged sword is an instrument like a surgeon's scalpel. It is not like a shotgun, which spreads over a large area and is not very powerful. This sword reveals what is carnal and what is truly spiritual, uncovering the thoughts and intents of the heart. Religious pride is exposed. Many do not truly desire the two-edged sword today.

Neither is there any creature that is not manifest in his sight: but all things are naked and opened unto the eyes of him with whom we have to do (Heb. 4:13).

Thy nakedness shall be uncovered, yea, thy shame shall be seen: I will take vengeance, and I will not meet thee as a man (Is. 47:3).

Come, see a man, which told me all things that ever I did: is not this the Christ? (John 4:29).

United Prophetic Revelation

But if all prophesy, and there come in one that believeth not, or one unlearned, he is convinced of all, he is judged of all: and thus are the secrets of his heart made manifest; and so falling down on his face he will worship God, and report that God is in you of a truth. How is it then, brethren? when ye come together, every one of you hath a psalm, hath a doctrine, hath a tongue, hath a revelation, hath an interpretation. Let all things be done unto edifying (1 Cor. 14:24–26).

Though I realize the dangers of what is called "body ministry," I believe in this form of worship. Manifestations may be brought forth in the flesh, but we are not to throw out things just because some have misused them. The key is to let each prophecy be judged. Does it build up or tear down? Does it bring life or death? We have encouraged this kind of worship for years and found it to be very effective when the saints' hearts are broken before God. However, prophecy will minister death if it is given in a proud and haughty spirit.

All Shall Prophesy

And it shall come to pass in the last days, saith God, I will pour out of my Spirit upon all flesh: and your sons and your daughters shall prophesy, and your young men shall see visions, and your old men shall dream dreams: and on my servants and on my handmaidens I will pour out in those days of my Spirit; and they shall prophesy (Acts 2:17–18).

Prophecy comes through a variety of manifestations: a poem, foretelling the future, preaching by inspiration, or holding the office of prophet. When it is actually operating in sons, daughters, old and young, male and female, it is a sign of the last days. When men try to organize it, it only brings confusion. But we are given very specific commands concerning the last days before the coming of our Lord.

Rejoice evermore. Pray without ceasing. In every thing give thanks: for this is the will of God in Christ Jesus concerning you. Quench not the Spirit. Despise not prophesyings. Prove all things; hold fast that which is good. Abstain from all appearance of evil. And the very God of peace sanctify you wholly; and I pray God your whole spirit and soul and body be preserved blameless unto the coming of our Lord Jesus Christ (1 Thess. 5:16–23).

Notice the simplicity of these commands: rejoice, pray, give thanks, let the Spirit flow, encourage prophecies, keep only what is proved good, and avoid evil appearances. The whole Church must be taught to judge and sift prophecy according the the Word of truth. There must be daily consistency which brings wholeness to spirit, soul and body. The two-edged sword must be in our hand. It must be reached for in faith. Daily practice is required in order to develop precision in the use of this instrument.

Remember, the weapon against the rulers of wickedness in high places is *united warfare*. Individual warfare has its place; but when encountering the united effort of Satan's army, we will not win without unity. Now is the time to pray and ask the Holy Spirit to free us from any spirit that is trespassing in the midst of the brethren.

Chapter Ten

UNDER THE FEET
OF THE CAPTAINS

A nd it came to pass, when they brought out those kings unto Joshua, that Joshua called for all the men of Israel, and said unto the captains of the men of war which went with him, Come near, put your feet upon the necks of these kings. And they came near, and put their feet upon the necks of them (Josh. 10:24).

The object of warfare is to make a public spectacle or open show of the enemy kings' and armies' defeat. All the armies of Israel watched while the captains put their feet on the kings' necks at Joshua's command.

And having disarmed the powers and authorities, he made a public spectacle of them, triumphing over them by the cross (Col. 2:15, NIV).

But thanks be to God, who always leads us in triumphal procession in Christ and through us spreads everywhere the fragrance of the knowledge of him (2 Cor. 2:14, NIV).

Triumph and victory are two different things. Jesus achieved victory through His death and resurrection. The Church has been called to make a public display of this spiritual truth. The new covenant ministry of signs, wonders and miracles publicly embarrasses the wicked rulers of darkness.

Captains And Apostles

Jesus was the first Apostle to the Church who was confirmed publicly by demonstrations of the Holy Spirit.

Wherefore, holy brethren, partakers of the heavenly calling, consider the Apostle and High Priest of our profession, Christ Jesus (Heb. 3:1).

Paul's ministry as an apostle was confirmed through demonstrations of power.

And my speech and my preaching was not with enticing words of man's wisdom, but in demonstration of the Spirit and of power: that your faith should not stand in the wisdom of men, but in the power of God (1 Cor. 2:4–5).

A new boldness is coming to the Church, as it recognizes apostolic authority. The Church is encouraged by a display of authority over the enemy. Along with signs and wonders, supernatural patience must be demonstrated.

Truly the signs of an apostle were wrought among you in all patience, in signs, and wonders, and mighty deeds (2 Cor. 12:12).

Because of the signs and wonders in the book of Acts, the word *magnified* was used to describe the response of the people to the apostles.

And by the hands of the apostles were many signs and wonders wrought among the people. . .the people magnified them (Acts 5:12, 13).

This does not mean the apostles were worshipped, but they were highly esteemed because of their ministry.

> **And we beseech you, brethren, to know them which labour among you, and are over you in the Lord, and admonish you: and to esteem them very highly in love for their work's sake (1 Thess. 5:12–13).**

The position of captain under Joshua is a type for the apostolic ministry of the New Testament Church. The apostle usually experiences the good and bad before the rest of the flock. He is the one who is up front in battle. Though not necessarily spiritually stronger than the rest of the flock, the anointing of authority accompanies his calling.

I am not saying it is impossible for a person who is not an apostle to occasionally have signs follow him; but generally speaking, there will not be a consistency of signs unless there is a spiritual calling to go as a messenger in a foundational calling.

I am sharing this to free you from condemnation that those who do not understand have heaped on the Church. While some reasons for not experiencing signs regularly could be doubt, fear or lack of faith, it could also be that your particular calling does not require as much demonstration of the supernatural as do other callings.

First Apostles, Secondly Prophets

> **And God hath set some in the church, first apostles, secondarily prophets, thirdly teachers, after that miracles, then gifts of healings, helps, governments, diversities of tongues (1 Cor. 12:28).**

> **Now therefore ye are no more strangers and foreigners, but fellow citizens with the saints, and of the household of God; and are built upon the foundation of the apostles and prophets, Jesus Christ himself being the chief corner stone (Eph. 2:19–20).**

While both the prophet and the apostle build the spiritual foundation of the Church, the apostle must do the initial work of ground-breaking. We might say the prophet pours the cement after the apostle has chosen the site and begun the digging process.

The Seventy Sent Out With Signs

After these things the Lord appointed other seventy also, and sent them two and two before his face into every city and place, whither he himself would come. Therefore said he unto them. . . heal the sick that are therein, and say unto them, The kingdom of God is come nigh unto you. . .. And the seventy returned again with joy, saying, Lord, even the devils are subject unto us through thy name (Luke 10:1–2, 9, 17).

The main purpose of this initial sending was to demonstrate authority over devils, with signs and wonders as a banner heralding the message of the kingdom of God: Satan is now a defeated foe, and it is time to walk forward in faith.

And he said unto them, I beheld Satan as lightning fall from heaven. Behold, I give unto you power to tread on serpents and scorpions, and over all the power of the enemy: and nothing shall by any means hurt you. Notwithstanding in this rejoice not, that the spirits are subject unto you; but rather rejoice, because your names are written in heaven. In that hour Jesus rejoiced in spirit, and said, I thank thee, O Father, Lord of heaven and earth, that thou hast hid these things from the wise and prudent, and hast revealed them unto babes: even so, Father; for so it seemed good in thy sight (Luke 10:18–21).

The Greek word for "rejoiced" is *agalliao*. Its root

meaning is "to jump for joy; exult, to be exceedingly glad, and exceedingly joyful." Jesus did this by the anointing of the Holy Spirit as a triumphant act of faith. He not only walked on devils, He danced on them.

Often leaders sit on the platform during a church service religiously "stiff and starchy," yet they preach liberty to the audience. This doesn't work. A sign of strong leadership is liberty in worship. The members will only be as free as the leaders who set the example. This kind of childlike rejoicing binds the ruler spirits of religious pride.

Apostles, The Feet Of The Body

Feet are part of the body of Christ. Other parts are hands, ears and eyes. But Jesus is the Head.

For the body is not one member, but many. If the foot shall say, Because I am not the hand, I am not of the body; is it therefore not of the body? And if the ear shall say, Because I am not the eye, I am not of the body; is it therefore not of the body? If the whole body were an eye, where were the hearing? If the whole were hearing, where were the smelling? But now hath God set the members every one of them in the body, as it hath pleased him. And if they were all one member, where were the body? But now are they many members, yet but one body. And the eye cannot say unto the hand, I have no need of thee: nor again the head to the feet, I have no need of you (1 Cor. 12:14–21).

The word *apostle* to some people identifies an exalted position in the body. But I suggest that the feet of the natural body may better describe the role of the apostle than any other member. In the following verses Paul describes himself:

For I am the least of the apostles, that am not meet to be called an apostle, because I persecuted the church of God (1 Cor. 15:9).

Unto me, who am less than the least of all saints, is this grace given, that I should preach among the Gentiles the unsearchable riches of Christ (Eph. 3:8).

The first qualification of a leader is to be poor in spirit like Paul. Then demonstration of signs will not cause him to be puffed up with pride.

Submitting To Instruction

If we expect the devils to flee, the first step in apostolic calling is to humble ourselves at the feet of our Lord and submit to His ways for cleansing of hands, heart and mind.

Submit yourselves therefore to God. Resist the devil, and he will flee from you. Draw nigh to God, and he will draw nigh to you. Cleanse your hands, ye sinners; and purify your hearts, ye double minded (James 4:7–8).

God's People Under Authority Have Authority

Demon-controlled kings of nations, states, cities, congregations and families bow at the feet of God's covenant people who humble themselves at His feet.

Who raised up the righteous man from the east, called him to his foot, gave the nations before him, and made him rule over kings? he gave them as the dust to his sword, and as driven stubble to his bow (Is. 41:2).

For he bringeth down them that dwell on high; the lofty city, he layeth it low; he layeth it low, even to the ground; he bringeth it even to the dust. The foot shall tread it down, even the feet of the poor, and the steps of the needy (Is. 26:5–6).

Blessed are the poor in spirit; for theirs is the kingdom of heaven (Matt. 5:3).

Kingdom power is the highest of all authority. The name of Jesus is higher than any name.

Thou hast put all things in subjection under his feet. For in that he put all in subjection under him, he left nothing that is not put under him (Heb. 2:8).

Principality, Power, Might And Dominion

Which he wrought in Christ, when he raised him from the dead, and set him at his own right hand in the heavenly places, far above all principality, and power, and might, and dominion, and every name that is named, not only in this world, but also in that which is to come: and hath put all things under his feet, and gave him to be the head over all things to the church, which is his body, the fulness of him that filleth all in all (Eph. 1:20–23).

The Greek word for principality is *ache*—a military term that means "rank in authority." The army of Jesus Christ outranks any other. Through Christ, we have greater authority than any demonic power. Power is *exousia* in Greek; it speaks of "superhuman ability, force, influence or jurisdiction." Might is *dunamai*—"availability and strength of the power source." Dominion is *kuriotes* in Greek; it means "rulers or governments." The word for name—*onomo*—as used in these scriptures, refers to the "character of the authority." For the believer, knowing the character of God causes bold faith to arise for warfare.

A person with the "captain calling" will be consistently taking new territory through Jesus Christ, our triumphant Lord and King.

Chapter Eleven

THE FIGHT OF FAITH

A nd Joshua said unto them, Fear not, nor be dismayed, be strong and of good courage: for thus shall the Lord do to all your enemies against whom ye fight (Josh. 10:25).

Every promise has conditions. The condition mentioned here is "*if* you will fight." For example: In order to receive healing, even medical science agrees that the patient's willingness to fight against sickness and disease is vital to recovery. Many times we fight, but in the flesh. We must fight the fight of faith.

Fear, Discouragement And Passivity

Three ruler spirits in any battle are fear, discouragement and passivity. These hinder spiritual demonstrations of strength and courage which arise from the heart. They are all strongholds of the mind. Our part is not only to defeat the enemy of "natural circumstances," but also to arise and be victorious in the battlefield in the mind.

Fear, dismay and passivity unite together as the

kings did in Joshua 10. It is not necessary to discern where one leaves off and the other begins. They dovetail, as do many of the gifts of the Holy Spirit.

Most of us recognize fear, but dismay is more subtle. *Dismay* means "to break down under confusion and fear," and "to abolish or abort the Word of God." God cannot help a fleeing army.

Passivity means "to offer no resistance, nor react to external influences; to be lacking in initiative and drive." Passivity says, "There's no need to even try." Dismay says, "I've tried it and it didn't work." Faith says, "There's no stopping until the enemy is completely destroyed."

In Paul's writing to Timothy, he exhorted him to hold fast to sound words, which means to get a wrestler's grip on truth.

Hold fast the form of sound words, which thou hast heard of me, in faith and love which is in Christ Jesus (2 Tim. 1:13).

The fight of faith begins with confession of an eternal truth.

Fight the good fight of faith, lay hold on eternal life, whereunto thou art also called, and hast professed a good profession before many witnesses (1 Tim. 6:12).

The word fight in the Greek is *agonizomia,* meaning "to struggle for the prize; to accomplish something." Our eyes must be on the goal instead of on the enemy.

Remember, Satan and his devils love the spotlight. This is why Jude wrote that we should not bring a slanderous accusation against the devil, but instead say, "The Lord rebuke you."

Yet Michael the archangel, when contending with the devil he disputed about the body of Moses, durst not bring against him a railing accusation, but said, The Lord rebuke thee (Jude 9).

I don't want to be legalistic about words, but we can't improve on what our Lord Jesus has already done. Our need is to build up our faith through praying in the Holy Ghost.

But ye, beloved, building up yourselves on your most holy faith, praying in the Holy Ghost (Jude 20).

For with stammering lips and another tongue will he speak to this people. To whom he said, This is the rest wherewith ye may cause the weary to rest; and this is the refreshing: yet they would not hear (Is. 28:11–12).

The Goal Is Rest

Victory is to enter into rest—knowing from the heart that Jesus has won the battle for us through His work at the cross and His resurrection. The struggle in our minds is to accept the truth that our service to Him in ministry is also accomplished.

Let us labour therefore to enter into that rest, lest any man fall after the same example of unbelief (Heb. 4:11).

In Hebrews 11, we see all the struggles of old covenant prophets and prophetesses; but the key to this chapter can be found in the last two verses:

And these all, having obtained a good report through faith, received not the promise: God having provided some better thing for us, that they without us should not be made perfect (Heb. 11:39–40).

Through the new and better covenant, we enter into the labor of Jesus and rest from the struggles the Old Testament prophets endured to receive a good report. Those who come to Him in meekness and learn that He bore the yoke of the law for us will enter into that rest. However, this does not relieve us of the command to fight the fight of faith.

Come unto me, all ye that labour and are heavy laden, and I will give you rest. Take my yoke upon you, and learn of me; for I am meek and lowly in heart: and ye shall find rest unto your souls. For my yoke is easy, and my burden is light (Matt. 11:28–30).

Faith In The Blood Covenant Ends Striving In The Flesh

For men verily swear by the greater: and an oath for confirmation is to them an end of all strife. Wherein God, willing more abundantly to shew unto the heirs of promise the immutability of his counsel, confirmed it by an oath (Heb. 6:16–17).

Many ministers have gone to heaven early because they did not relax while doing spiritual warfare. Working ourselves into an emotional or physical frenzy is a tip-off to the devil that faith in the finished work of Jesus is not being exercised. The enemy knows that exhaustion will prevent us from fighting. Then, because of dismay, Satan eventually wins.

To be attacked by fear, discouragement and fatigue is normal while doing spiritual warfare of any kind. The key is that we must focus on Jesus, the Living Word, and worship Him until we are renewed. We must have faith in the covenant promise, "I will give you rest every time!"

Exhortation Against Fear

Leaders must exhort the army that refreshment and help is on the way. We must say, "Don't cave in to fear."

Say to them that are of a fearful heart, Be strong, fear not: behold, your God will come with

vengeance, even God with a recompence; he will come and save you. Then the eyes of the blind shall be opened, and the ears of the deaf shall be unstopped. Then shall the lame man leap as an hart, and the tongue of the dumb sing: for in the wilderness shall waters break out, and streams in the desert (Is. 35:4–6).

And it shall be, when ye are come nigh unto the battle, that the priest shall approach and speak unto the people, and shall say unto them, Hear, O Israel, ye approach this day unto battle against your enemies: let not your hearts faint, fear not, and do not tremble, neither be ye terrified because of them; for the Lord your God is he that goeth with you, to fight for you against your enemies, to save you (Deut. 20:2–4).

Jesus Commanded, "Fear Not"

Jesus practiced leadership this way. If we follow our emotions as leaders, we will be apt to sympathize or agree with the fears of the troops. This is the greatest mistake a leader can make—in the family or the Church.

And he saith unto them, Why are ye fearful, O ye of little faith? Then he arose, and rebuked the winds and the sea; and there was a great calm (Matt. 8:26).

And when the disciples saw him walking on the sea, they were troubled, saying, It is a spirit; and they cried out for fear (Matt. 14:26).

While he yet spake, there came from the ruler of the synagogue's house certain which said, Thy daughter is dead: why troublest thou the Master any further? As soon as Jesus heard the word that was spoken, he saith unto the ruler of the synagogue, Be not afraid, only believe (Mark 5:35–36).

Peace I leave with you, my peace I give unto you: not as the world giveth, give I unto you. Let not your heart be troubled, neither let it be afraid (John 14:27).

Fear Is Contagious

Fear is contagious and cannot be tolerated in the army of God. It is a disease that can spread like small pox, measles or the common cold. The immune system must be built up before going into battle. A wise leader will give priority to "preventive maintenance" rather than "crisis management" in his church or family.

And the officers shall speak further unto the people, and they shall say, What man is there that is fearful and fainthearted? let him go and return unto his house, lest his brethren's heart faint as well as his heart (Deut. 20:8).

Now therefore go to, proclaim in the ears of the people, saying, Whosoever is fearful and afraid, let him return and depart early from mount Gilead. And there returned of the people twenty and two thousand; and there remained ten thousand (Judg. 7:3).

Numbers Not As Important As Preparedness

We must remember it is not the number of spiritual warriors we have, but their victorious spirits that count. Fearing the size of the enemy army must be overcome by confessing that we fear only the Lord. This looses us from the bondage of fear.

Sanctify the Lord of hosts himself; and let him be your fear, and let him be your dread (Is. 8:13).

And fear not them which kill the body, but are not able to kill the soul: but rather fear him which is able to destroy both soul and body in hell (Matt. 10:28).

Elisha exhorted his servant not to fear the natural revelation of his eyes, but prayed to have his eyes see only the truth of the matter.

Fear not: for they that be with us are more than they that be with them. And Elisha prayed, and said, Lord, I pray thee, open his eyes, that he may see. And the Lord opened the eyes of the young man; and he saw: and, behold, the mountain was full of horses and chariots of fire round about Elisha (2 Kings 6:16–17).

Up-Front Confession

A confession must be made before the battle begins that regardless of the outcome, we will lean on the Lord of Hosts, our strength and courage. We will be amazed how courage to do battle will supernaturally arise. We will praise and worship our God because He is fighting through these bodies of clay.

Though an host should encamp against me, my heart shall not fear: though war should rise against me, in this will I be confident (Ps. 27:3).

Therefore will we not fear, though the earth be removed, and though the mountains be carried into the midst of the sea (Ps. 46:2).

In God I will praise his word, in God I have put my trust; I will not fear what flesh can do unto me (Ps. 56:4).

The Lord is on my side; I will not fear: what can man do unto me? (Ps. 118:6).

Love is the exact opposite of fear. An amazing miracle happens when we're totally wrapped up in the love of Jesus, with no fear of death.

There is no fear in love; but perfect love casteth out fear: because fear hath torment. He that feareth is not made perfect in love (1 John 4:18).

For God hath not given us the spirit of fear; but of power, and of love, and of a sound mind (2 Tim. 1:7).

And I say unto you my friends, Be not afraid of them that kill the body, and after that have no more that they can do (Luke 12:4).

The War-horse

In the book of Job we find a description of the horse, an animal specially trained for battle in the king's army. It has no fear of battle. On the contrary, it seems to enjoy a fierce encounter, because to fight is to win. There is no thought of defeat in this war-horse because he has been bred and trained for war.

The Church must be of the same spirit through the overcoming Spirit of Christ in us. He has defeated every enemy and has entered into rest beside the Father. We are seated with Him in heavenly places (see Eph. 1:3; 2:6). Our spiritual labor is to rise to that place.

Hast thou given the horse strength? hast thou clothed his neck with thunder? Canst thou make him afraid as a grasshopper? the glory of his nostrils is terrible. He paweth in the valley, and rejoiceth in his strength: he goeth on to meet the armed men. He mocketh at fear, and is not affrighted; neither turneth he back from the sword. The quiver rattleth against him, the glittering spear and the shield. He swalloweth the ground with fierceness and rage: neither believeth he that it is the sound of the trumpet. He saith among the trumpets, Ha, ha; and he smelleth the battle afar off, the thunder of the captains, and the shouting (Job 39:19–25).

May each of us have the assurance Paul had when he wrote these words near the end of his time on earth:

I have fought a good fight, I have finished my course, I have kept the faith: Henceforth there is laid up for me a crown of righteousness, which the Lord, the righteous judge, shall give me at that day: and not to me only, but unto all them also that love his appearing (2 Tim. 4:7–8).

Chapter Twelve

THE CROSS AND THE GRAVE

A nd afterward Joshua smote them, and slew them, and hanged them on five trees: and they were hanging upon the trees until the evening (Josh. 10:26).

This chapter may be the most important one of all. Without the message of death on the cross and resurrection from the dead, there is no hope of overcoming the enemy and receiving everlasting life. Jesus was tried and crucified as a wicked king—a ruler of darkness of the world and spiritual wickedness in high places. Though he was innocent of their charges he bore the reproach that his church might have authority over wicked kings of spiritual darkness.

Crucified As A Wicked King

And when they had platted a crown of thorns, they put it upon his head, and a reed in his right hand: and they bowed the knee before him, and mocked him, saying, Hail, King of the Jews!. . . He saved others; himself he cannot save. If he be the

King of Israel, let him now come down from the cross, and we will believe him (Matt. 27:29, 42).

And he made his grave with the wicked, and with the rich in his death; because he had done no violence, neither was any deceit in his mouth (Isa. 53:9).

Therefore will I divide him a portion with the great, and he shall divide the spoil with the strong; because he hath poured out his soul unto death: and he was numbered with the transgressors; and he bare the sin of many, and made intercession for the transgressors (Is. 53:12).

Jesus allowed Himself to be mocked like a rich and wicked king. At the same time, He made intercession for His Church. Therefore, through faith in His blood we are delivered from the bondage of rulers of spiritual wickedness.

Every ruler demon of spiritual wickedness attacked the body and mind of Jesus as He hung on the cross. The scene was so ugly that the Father momentarily turned His face away from Him, lest He judge Him. Jesus covered every ruler of darkness with His own blood, so the Father could again look upon Him. When the Father looked again, all He could see was righteous, sinless blood. This is our position as believers in Christ today.

The Grave

And it came to pass at the time of the going down of the sun, that Joshua commanded, and they took them down off the trees, and cast them into the cave wherein they had been hid, and laid great stones in the cave's mouth, which remain until this very day (Josh. 10:27).

The bodies of the five kings are a type for the old

sinful nature of man who has been crucified with Christ. The man of sin is left in the grave. Jesus arose in His new spiritual body, but the cursed uncircumcised fleshly nature of man did not arise. So do we arise from the waters of baptism.

Buried with him in baptism, wherein also ye are risen with him through the faith of the operation of God, who hath raised him from the dead. And you, being dead in your sins and the uncircumcision of your flesh, hath he quickened together with him, having forgiven you all trespasses (Col. 2:12–13).

The rock which human men rolled over the door is a type of the gates of Hades or the grave. Jesus spoke about this in Matthew 16:18. It could not bind Jesus because of the power of the Word which said He would rise again.

And shall deliver him to the Gentiles to mock, and to scourge, and to crucify him: and the third day he shall rise again (Matt. 20:19).

The Risen Christ

If the Spirit of him who raised Jesus from the dead is living in you, he who raised Christ from the dead will also give life to your mortal bodies through his Spirit, who lives in you (Rom. 8:11, NIV).

The Spirit of truth raises believers to be seated in Christ, far above principalities and wicked powers. All ruler spirits of wickedness are still chained in darkness with the rock of revelation until this day.

And the angels which kept not their first estate, but left their own habitation, he hath reserved in everlasting chains under darkness unto the judgment of the great day (Jude 6).

Satan and his devils have authority to function

only where there are pockets of darkness or secret rooms in our spiritual house which have not been opened to the Lord through repentance.

I am come a light into the world, that whosoever believeth on me should not abide in darkness (John 12:46).

Chapter Thirteen

JESUS IN THE MIDST
(THE MEDIATOR OF THE COVENANT)

Although some of our problems seem complex at times, God's solutions are uncomplicated. The question is whether there is a clean or unclean spirit between us. Let us focus on the Holy (clean) Spirit in the midst. This is none other than Jesus, the blood covenant Mediator.

Throughout the Old Testament there is one main theme—the blood covenant. This helps us understand the new and better covenant of which Jesus is the mediator. In Jewish culture, absolutely sure and unchangeable agreements were made by "cutting" a covenant.

In Hebrew, the word for covenant is *beriyth*, which means "to cut." Covenant is made by passing between pieces of flesh.

How Can I Know?

In Genesis 15, God cut covenant with Abram. He had believed God and had been counted righteous; yet he asked how he could know for sure that he would receive the inheritance that God had promised to him.

And he said, Lord God, whereby shall I know that I shall inherit it? And he said unto him, Take me an heifer of three years old, and a she goat of three years old, and a ram of three years old, and a turtle dove, and a young pigeon. And he took unto him all these, and divided them in the midst, and laid each piece one against another: but the birds divided he not. And when the fowls came down upon the carcasses, Abram drove them away (Gen. 15:8–11).

God was communicating on Abram's level, since he had evidently practiced covenant-cutting all his life. He had seen this practiced between two individuals many times; but now Almighty God was, for the first time, cutting covenant with a man. So to answer Abram's question about how he could know, God showed him the blood sacrifice with demonstrations of power in the midst.

Life In The Blood Sacrifice

After Abram had cut the animals in half, the birds came and tried to steal the blood sacrifice. The birds represent the devil, who seeks to devour the seed of truth concerning blood sacrifice.

And it came to pass, as he sowed, some fell by the way side, and the fowls of the air came and devoured it up (Mark 4:4).

The thief cometh not, but for to steal, and to kill, and to destroy: I am come that they might have life, and that they might have it more abundantly (John 10:10).

If the devil can steal the truth about the blood sacrifice from us and cause us to base our faith on dead works, he can steal our very life in the blood of Christ.

117

For the life of the flesh is in the blood: and I have given it to you upon the altar to make an atonement for your souls: for it is the blood that maketh an atonement for the soul (Lev. 17:11).

It is the believer's responsibility to protect, or hold fast to, his confession of the blood. To speak of blood is repulsive to the flesh; therefore, many who believe in the blood of Jesus will not testify and speak of it.

Testimony Of The Blood

And they overcame him by the blood of the Lamb, and by the word of their testimony; and they loved not their lives unto the death (Rev. 12:11).

Overcomers must verbally profess the life that is in the blood covenant of Jesus.

Seeing then that we have a great high priest, that is passed into the heavens, Jesus the Son of God, let us hold fast our profession (Heb. 4:14).

The Hebrew word for profession is *homologeo*, which means "assent, covenant, acknowledge, confession, give thanks and promise."

The children of Israel were commanded to kill an animal and take the blood in a bowl and paint their doorposts with it. The blood was of no benefit until it was *applied* to the doorpost. So it is with the blood of Jesus and our confession of His blood. Merely giving mental assent to a truth does not bind the enemy.

On several occasions, my wife and I have heard demons speak through a person's mouth and beg us not to say any more about the blood. In every instance, as we continued to declare the power of the blood aloud, deliverance came.

Blameless

We are dealing with the master accuser who enjoys getting God's righteous children in a judicial type of position. He insists that we plead either innocent or guilty. If we plead innocent, he draws attention to our past mistakes; if we plead guilty, he demands we pay the full penalty. So how shall we plead? The only response that silences the accuser is to call upon the power of the blood of Christ, hence the expression, "I plead the blood of Jesus". We are blameless in the eyes of the Father because Jesus paid the debt for our sins with His own precious blood.

That ye may be blameless and harmless, the sons of God, without rebuke, in the midst of a crooked and perverse nation, among whom ye shine as lights in the world (Phil. 2:15).

And the very God of peace sanctify you wholly; and I pray God your whole spirit and soul and body be preserved blameless unto the coming of our Lord Jesus Christ (1 Thess. 5:23).

Curse of Sin Covered by Blood

When Jesus' blood was shed, every inch of His body—from the top of His head to the bottom of His feet—was covered by His blood. He had taken every curse upon Himself and appeared as a serpent on a pole.

And as Moses lifted up the serpent in the wilderness, even so must the Son of man be lifted up (Jn. 3:14).

He hath made him to be sin for us who knew no sin; that we might be made the righteousness of God in him (II Cor. 5:21).

Christ hath redeemed us from the curse of the

law, being made a curse for us: for it is written, cursed is everyone that hangeth on a tree (Gal. 3:13).

When we picture the scene at the cross, we must see all our sins covered—hidden from the eyes of the Father—under that blood. Before the work of the cross was totally finished, the Father turned His face away and chose not to look on our sin. This is when Jesus cried, "My God, My God, why have You forsaken Me?" (Ps. 22:1, NKJV). The father was keeping the covenant promise to remember his church as righteous and not as sinners. For I will be merciful to their unrighteousness, and their sins and their iniquities will I remember no more (Heb. 8:11). After the piercing of Jesus' side by the Roman soldier's spear, the Father looked again and saw nothing but blood.

Deuteronomy 28 spells out the blessings and cursings of obedience or disobedience to the law. The curses include being destroyed by every possible enemy one can imagine—sickness, poverty, loss of wife and children, insanity, loneliness, defeat....

When we read these curses we should look at the sacrifice of Christ as an insurance policy. When we are condemned by the letter of the law and offered any of these curses our reply must be, "I'm covered by the blood." It is not necessary to explain to the devil what the blood means, because he knows this truth very well. One should never have a lengthy conversation with the devil.

When a person has an automobile accident and has insurance, he can confidently say, "I'm covered." How much more covered are we when we have a covenant in which Jesus has performed perfectly on our behalf?

The Performance of the Covenant

And when the sun was going down, a deep sleep fell upon Abram; and, lo, an horror of great darkness fell upon him (Gen. 15:12).

Abram was put into a deep sleep, much like Adam when his bride was brought forth through the cutting and shedding of his blood. Coequal participation was customary in cutting a covenant, but now God must totally perform this covenant without any assistance from Abram. This was a new covenant of righteousness—a free gift.

But not as the offence, so also is the free gift. For if through the offence of one many be dead, much more the grace of God, and the gift by grace, which is by one man, Jesus Christ, hath abounded unto many. And not as it was by one that sinned, so is the gift: for the judgment was by one to condemnation, but the free gift is of many offences unto justification. For if by one man's offence death reigned by one; much more they which receive abundance of grace and of the gift of righteousness shall reign in life by one, Jesus Christ (Rom. 5:15–17).

Jesus perfectly performed the new covenant in our behalf to free us from every enemy so that we can serve Him without fear, in holiness and righteousness all the days of our lives.

That we should be saved from our enemies, and from the hand of all that hate us; to perform the mercy promised to our fathers, and to remember his holy covenant; the oath which he sware to our father Abraham, that he would grant unto us, that we being delivered out of the hand of our enemies might serve him without fear, in holiness and righteousness before him, all the days of our life (Luke 1:71–75).

In his helpless state Abram saw Jesus passing through death on his behalf.

Holy Spirit And Fire In The Midst

And it came to pass, that, when the sun went down, and it was dark, behold a smoking furnace, and a burning lamp that passed between these pieces (Gen. 15:17).

Your father Abraham rejoiced to see my day: and he saw it, and was glad (John 8:56).

Abram saw Jesus, the Mediator, in the midst of His spiritual body. What he saw had all the ingredients of the glorious Church—the blood-covered flesh with Holy Spirit manifestations in the midst.

The furnace represents the refinement that comes through the baptism of fire. Like the three Hebrew children of Daniel 3, the furnace will deliver us from our bonds and allow us to walk with the Son of God.

I commanded your fathers in the day that I brought them forth out of the land of Egypt, from the iron furnace, saying, Obey my voice, and do them, according to all which I command you: so shall ye be my people, and I will be your God (Jer. 11:4).

Behold, I have refined thee, but not with silver; I have chosen thee in the furnace of affliction (Is. 48:10).

The burning lamp represents the Spirit of Truth that reveals, guides and releases from condemnation.

Thy word is a lamp unto my feet, and a light unto my path. I have sworn, and I will perform it, that I will keep thy righteous judgments (Ps. 119:105–106).

No unclean religious spirit can dwell where the spiritual lamp and furnace mediate in the midst of the body and all flesh is covered by the blood of Jesus.

The Lord Be Between Us

Remember the cutting of covenants between David and Jonathan and Jacob and Laban? The end result in both instances was agreement and a statement—based on blood—that the Lord would be the mediator between them.

And Jonathan said to David, Go in peace, forasmuch as we have sworn both of us in the name of the Lord, saying, The Lord be between me and thee, and between my seed and thy seed for ever. And he arose and departed: and Jonathan went into the city (1 Sam. 20:42).

Lively Stones as a Token of the Covenant Made Between Jacob and Laban

And Laban said, This heap is a witness between me and thee this day. Therefore was the name of it called Galeed; and Mizpah: for he said, The Lord watch between me and thee, when we are absent one from another. If thou shalt afflict my daughters, or if thou shalt take other wives beside my daughters, no man is with us; see, God is witness betwixt me and thee. And Laban said to Jacob, Behold this heap, and behold this pillar, which I have cast betwixt me and thee; this heap be witness, and this pillar be witness, that I will not pass over this heap to thee, and that thou shalt not pass over this heap and this pillar unto me, for harm. The God of Abraham, and the God of Nahor, the God of their father, judge betwixt us. And Jacob sware by the fear of his father Isaac (Gen. 31:48–53). The work of mediation is accomplished by the united reflection of Jesus through the various different gifts and ministries which God has set in the midst of his church today.

But now hath he obtained a more excellent ministry, by how much also he is the mediator of a better covenant, which was established upon better promises (Heb. 8:6).

And You Shall Know Me

Let's go back to the original question of how we can be sure of our inheritance. The Holy Spirit causes those who believe and confess the new and better covenant to "know," as a wife knows her husband.

For this is the covenant that I will make with the house of Israel after those days, saith the Lord; I will put my laws into their mind, and write them in their hearts: and I will be to them a God, and they shall be to me a people: and they shall not teach every man his neighbour, and every man his brother, saying, Know the Lord: for all shall know me, from the least to the greatest. For I will be merciful to their unrighteousness, and their sins and their iniquities will I remember no more (Heb. 8:10–12).

To know someone in this sense is more than a casual acquaintance; it is an intimate relationship. This kind of knowing God is, in a spiritual sense, much like the intimacy a husband and wife share in the natural. There is an overshadowing and the seed is planted, which grows and produces children, to the glory of the Father.

Overshadowed By Power

Consider the virgin Mary, who asked much the same question as Abram did. She questioned how this could be, since she had never known (been intimate with) a man. The answer came: the Holy Ghost would come upon her and the power of the Highest would overshadow her (see Luke 1:34–35).

In the case of Abraham and Sarah, Isaac was God's promised child to them. Instead of waiting for God's promise to come to pass, because of her barrenness, Sarah suggested Abraham have a child by Hagar, and Ishmael was born. Ishmael is a type for spiritual bondage in the Church today—products of religious spirits and not of Spirit-imparted faith.

Cast Out The Spirit Of Bondage

Now we, brethren, as Isaac was, are the children of promise. But as then he that was born after the flesh persecuted him that born after the Spirit, even so it is now. Nevertheless what saith the scripture? Cast out the bondwoman and her son: for the son of the bondwoman shall not be heir with the son of the freewoman. So then, brethren, we are not children of the bondwoman, but of the free (Gal. 4:28–31).

Notice the terminology "cast out the bondwoman and her son." This tells me we are dealing with a devil called religious bondage, which has bewitched the minds of those who were once free. It must be cast out with the mighty weapons of the Holy Spirit.

O foolish Galatians, who hath bewitched you, that ye should not obey the truth, before whose eyes Jesus Christ hath been evidently set forth, crucified among you? (Gal. 3:1).

The answer to the problem of religious bondage is simply this: where there is a flow of the Spirit of life in the midst of the body, there can be no dwelling place for ruler spirits of darkness and death. The blood, the furnace, and the lamp purge the very heart of the body of Christ on earth as it has been done in heaven.

In all my life, I have never run across one person
who is against unity. Everyone desires unity.
Everything humanly possible has been done to achieve
it. Why is there so little true unity? Religious spirits in
the midst.

Right now, receive your free gift of unity through
the blood of Jesus Christ, and pray with me:

> Ruler spirits of darkness,
>> the light has shone upon you!
> You are bound with the rock of revelation
>> in the name of Jesus!
> The lines of communication have been broken
>> between you and your fleeing and
>> defeated congregation of devils.
> We, by the authority of Jesus Christ,
>> do eradicate and exterminate the hosts of hell.
> We, the army of the Lord of Hosts,
>> do now completely destroy your ranks.
> And the gates of hell shall not prevail against
>> the blood-bought Church,
>>> which is built on the Rock. Amen!